shakespeare's
the tempest

shakespeare's
the tempest

harold bloom

riverhead books
new york

THE BERKLEY PUBLISHING GROUP
Published by the Penguin Group
Penguin Group (USA) Inc.
375 Hudson Street, New York, New York 10014, USA
Penguin Group (Canada), 10 Alcorn Avenue, Toronto, Ontario M4V 3B2, Canada
(a division of Pearson Penguin Canada Inc.)
Penguin Books Ltd., 80 Strand, London WC2R 0RL, England
Penguin Group Ireland, 25 St. Stephen's Green, Dublin 2, Ireland (a division of Penguin Books Ltd.)
Penguin Group (Australia), 250 Camberwell Road, Camberwell, Victoria 3124, Australia
(a division of Pearson Australia Group Pty. Ltd.)
Penguin Books India Pvt. Ltd., 11 Community Centre, Panchsheel Park, New Delhi—110 017, India
Penguin Group (NZ), cnr Airborne and Rosedale Roads, Albany, Auckland 1310, New Zealand
(a division of Pearson New Zealand Ltd.)
Penguin Books (South Africa) (Pty.) Ltd., 24 Sturdee Avenue, Rosebank, Johannesburg 2196,
South Africa

Penguin Books Ltd., Registered Offices: 80 Strand, London WC2R 0RL, England

PRINTING HISTORY
First Riverhead trade paperback edition: April 2005

Library of Congress Cataloging-in-Publication Data

Bloom, Harold.
    Shakespeare's The tempest / Harold Bloom.— 1st Riverhead trade pbk. ed.
      p. cm.
    "The essay 'The tempest' was previously published as part of Shakespeare : the invention of the
human, by Harold Bloom"—T.p. verso.
    Includes the full text of the play, with editorial revisions by Harold Bloom.
    ISBN 1-59448-077-X
    1. Shakespeare, William, 1564–1616. Tempest.   2. Survival after airplane accidents,
shipwrecks, etc.—Drama.   3. Fathers and daughters—Drama.   4. Magicians—Drama.
5. Castaways—Drama.   6. Tragicomedy.   I. Shakespeare, Willim, 1564–1616. Tempest.
II. Title

PR2833.B55 2005
822.3'3—dc22

                            2004065074

PRINTED IN THE UNITED STATES OF AMERICA

10 9 8 7 6 5 4 3 2 1

contents

The text of *The Tempest*, including the synopsis, is that of the old Cambridge Edition (1893), as edited by William Aldis Wright. I am grateful to Brett Foster for indispensable advice upon the editorial revisions I have made in the text.

—Harold Bloom

harold bloom on
the tempest

Of all Shakespeare's plays, the two visionary comedies—*A Midsummer Night's Dream* and *The Tempest*—these days share the sad distinction of being the worst interpreted and performed. Erotomania possesses the critics and directors of the *Dream,* while ideology drives the bespoilers of *The Tempest*. Caliban, a poignant but cowardly (and murderous) half-human creature (his father a sea devil, whether fish or amphibian), has become an African-Caribbean heroic Freedom Fighter. This is not even a weak misreading; anyone who arrives at that view is simply not interested in reading the play at all. Marxists, multiculturalists, feminists, *nouveau* historicists—the usual suspects—know their causes but not Shakespeare's plays.

Because *The Tempest* (1611) was Shakespeare's last play without the collaboration of John Fletcher, and probably had been a success at the Globe, it heads off the First Folio, printed as the first of the comedies. We know that *The Tempest* was presented at the court of James I, which probably accounts for its masquelike features. The play is fundamentally plotless; its one outer event is the magically induced storm of the first scene, which rather oddly gives the play its title. If there is any literary source at all, it would be Montaigne's essay on the Cannibals, who are echoed in Caliban's name though not in his nature. Yet Montaigne, as in *Hamlet,* was more provocation than source, and Caliban is anything but a celebration of the natural man. *The Tempest* is neither a discourse on colonialism nor a mystical testament. It is a wildly experimental stage comedy, prompted ultimately, I suspect, by Marlowe's *Doctor Faustus.* Prospero, Shakespeare's magus, carries a name that is the Italian translation of Faustus, which is the Latin cognomen ("the favored one") that Simon Magus the Gnostic took when he went to Rome. With Ariel, a sprite or angel (the name is Hebrew for "the lion of God"), as his familiar rather than Marlowe's Mephistopheles, Prospero is Shakespeare's anti-Faust, and a final transcending of Marlowe.

Since Caliban, though he speaks only a hundred lines in *The Tempest,* has now taken over the play for so many, I will start with him here. His fortunes in stage history are instructive, and comfort me at our bad moment for *The Tempest.* In Davenant and Dryden's *The Enchanted Isle,* a musical revision that held the London stage on and off between 1667 and 1787, Caliban gets himself so drunk early on that he instigates no plot against Prospero. This Caliban (a different kind of travesty from our current noble rebel) for more than a century provided a prime role for singing comedians. In the High Romantic period, the prancing and yodeling yahoo finally was replaced by Shakespeare's poignant "savage and deformed slave." As the text suggests, Caliban was still represented as half amphibian, but peculiar transformations crowded after that: a snail on all fours, a gorilla, the Missing Link or ape man, and at last (London, 1951) a Neanderthal. In a ghastly Peter Brook version of the 1960s, which I gaped at unbelievingly, Caliban was Java Man, a ferocious primitive who accomplished the rape of Miranda, took over the island, and celebrated his triumph by bumbuggering

Prospero. Another modern tradition—now, of course, prevalent—has cast black actors in the role: Canada Lee, Earle Hyman, and James Earl Jones were among the early exemplars whom I saw. In 1970, Jonathan Miller was inspired to set the play in the age of Cortés and Pizarro, with Caliban as a South American Indian field hand, and Ariel as an Indian literate serf. That was bizarre enough to be entertaining, unlike George C. Wolfe's infuriating recent success, in which Caliban and Ariel, both black slaves, vied with one another in hating Prospero. Fashions tire; the early twenty-first century may still have mock scholars moaning about neocolonialism, but I assume that by then Caliban and Ariel will be extraterrestrials—perhaps they are already.

The critical tradition, until recently, has been far more perceptive than the directorial, as regards the role of Caliban. Dryden accurately observed that Shakespeare "created a person which was not in Nature." A character who is half-human cannot be a natural man, whether black, Indian, or Berber (the likely people of Caliban's mother, the Algerian witch Sycorax). Dr. Johnson, no sentimentalist, wrote of "the gloominess of his temper and the malignity of his purposes," while dismissing any notion that Caliban spoke a language of his own. In our century, the poet Auden blamed Prospero for corrupting Caliban, a simplistic judgment, but as always Auden on Shakespeare benefits us by his insight, here in the wonderful prose address "Caliban to the Audience," from *The Sea and the Mirror*. Perhaps because Shelley had identified with Ariel, Auden assimilates Caliban to himself:

And from this nightmare of public solitude, this everlasting Not Yet, what relief have you but in an ever giddier collective gallop, with bisson eye and bevel course, toward the grey horizon of the bleaker vision; what landmarks but the four dead rivers, the Joyless, the Flowing, the Mournful, and the Swamp of Tears, what goal but the Black Stone on which the bones are cracked, for only there in its cry of agony can your existence find at last an unequivocal meaning and your refusal to be yourself become a serious despair, the love nothing, the fear all?

This is primarily Auden on Auden, heavily influenced by Kierkegaard, but it catches Caliban's dilemma: "The love nothing, the fear all." Between Johnson and Auden on Caliban, the great figure is Browning, in his astonishing dramatic monologue "Caliban upon Setebos." Here the terrible psychic suffering brought about through the failed adoption of Caliban by Prospero is granted fuller expression than Shakespeare allowed:

> Himself peeped late, eyed Prosper at his books
> Careless and lofty, lord now of the isle:
> Vexed, 'stitched a book of broad leaves, arrow-shaped,
> Wrote thereon, he knows what, prodigious words;
> Has peeled a wand and called it by a name;
> Weareth at whiles for an enchanter's robe
> The eyed skin of a supple ocelot;
> And hath an ounce sleeker than youngling mole,
> A four-legged serpent he makes cower and couch,
> Now snarl, now hold its breath and mind his eye,
> And saith she is Miranda and my wife:
> Keeps for his Ariel a tall pouch-bill crane
> He bids go wade for fish and straight disgorge;
> Also a sea-beast, lumpish, which he snared,
> Blinded the eyes of, and brought somewhat tame,
> And split its toe-webs, and now pens the drudge
> In a hole o'the rock and calls him Caliban;
> A bitter heart that bides its time and bites.
> Plays thus at being Prosper in a way,
> Taketh his mirth with make-believes: so He.

As throughout Browning's poem, Caliban speaks of himself in the third person, except that the final "He" is Setebos, the god of the witch Sycorax. The lumpish sea beast, "a bitter heart that bides its time and bites," is a sick child's tortured plaything. Cast out by Prospero, Caliban bides his time but will be too fearful and inept to bite. What Browning sees is Caliban's essential childishness, a weak and plangent sensibility that cannot surmount its fall from the paradisal adoption by Prospero. Caliban's attempted rape of Miranda is readily explained away by his current academic admirers, but I wonder sometimes why feminist critics join in Caliban's defense. On this matter, the audience's perspective has to be that of Miranda and Prospero, and not Caliban's antic glee that, had he not been prevented, he would have peopled all the isle with Calibans. Half a Wild Man, half a sea beast, Caliban has his legitimate pathos, but he cannot be interpreted as being somehow admirable.

2

A play virtually plotless must center its interest elsewhere, yet Shakespeare in *The Tempest* seems more concerned with what Prospero might intimate than with the coldness of this anti-Faust's personality. Ariel also is more a figure of vast suggestiveness than a character possessing an inwardness available to us, except by glimpses. Part of *The Tempest*'s permanent fascination for so many playgoers and readers, in a myriad of national cultures, is its juxtaposition of a vengeful magus who turns to forgiveness, with a spirit of fire and air, and a half-human of earth and water. Prospero seems to incarnate a fifth element, similar to that of the Sufis, like himself descended from the ancient Hermetists. The art of Prospero controls nature, at least in the outward sense. Though his art ought also to teach Prospero an absolute self-control, he clearly has not attained this even as the play concludes. Prospero's Platonism is at best enigmatic; self-knowledge in Neo-Platonic tradition hardly should lead on to despair, and yet Prospero ends in a dark mode, particularly evident in the Epilogue that he speaks.

What was Shakespeare trying to do for himself as a playwright, if not necessarily as a person, by composing *The Tempest*? We can conclude reasonably that he did not intend this drama to be a final work. In 1611, Shakespeare was only forty-seven, and he did write substantial parts, at least, of three more plays: *Henry VIII,* the lost *Cardenio,* and *The Two Noble Kinsmen,* probably all with the collaboration of John Fletcher. Prospero is not more a representation of Shakespeare himself than Dr. Faustus was a self-portrait of Christopher Marlowe. Yet Romantic readers and playgoers felt otherwise, and I am still enough of a Late Romantic to wish to surmise what moved them to their extravagance.

There is an elliptical quality to *The Tempest* that suggests a more symbolic drama than Shakespeare actually wrote. Prospero, unlike Hamlet, does not end saying that he has something more to tell us, but that he must "let it be." We rightly feel that Hamlet could have told us something crucial about what he himself represented, could have plucked the heart out of his mystery, had he had the time and the inclination to do so. Prospero's seems a very different story of the self: Hamlet dies into the truth, while Prospero lives on in what may be a bewilderment or at least a puzzlement. Since Prospero's story is not tragic, but somehow comic, in the old sense of ending happily (or at least successfully), he appears to lose spiritual authority even as he regains political power. I am not suggesting that Prospero loses the prestige we generally ascribe to tragedy, and to Hamlet in particular. Rather, the authority of a counter-Faust, who could purchase knowledge at no spiritual cost, abandons Prospero. Leaving the enchanted isle is not in itself a loss for Prospero, but breaking his staff and drowning his book certainly constitute diminishments to the self. These emblems of purified magic were also the marks of exile: going home to rule Milan purchases restoration at a high price. Prospero, bidding farewell to his art, tells us that he even has raised the dead, a role that Christianity reserves for God and for Jesus. To be Duke of Milan is to be only another potentate; the abandoned art was so potent that politics is absurd in contrast.

The Tempest is more Ariel's play than Caliban's, and much more Prospero's. Indeed *Prospero* would be a far apter title than *The Tempest,* which turns me to what seems the play's true mystery: Why does it so slyly invoke the Faust story, only to transform legend beyond recognition? Simon Magus, according to Christian sources (no Gnostic ones being available), suffered the irony of being not "the favored one" at all when he went to Rome. In a contest with Christians, this first Faustus attempted levitation, and crashed down to his death. Most subsequent Fausts sell out to the Devil, and pay with spirit, the grandest exception being Goethe, for his Faust's soul is borne off to heaven by little boy angels whose chubby buttocks so intoxicate Mephistopheles with homoerotic lust that he notices too late the theft of his legitimate prize.

Prospero, the anti-Faust, with the angel Ariel for his familiar, has made a pact only with deep learning of the hermetic kind. Since Marlowe's Dr. Faustus was a failed scholar compared with Prospero, Shakespeare enjoys foregrounding an ironic contrast between his long-defunct rival's protagonist and the magus of *The Tempest.* Simon Magus was, like Jesus the Magician, a disciple of John the Baptist, and evidently resented that he was not preferred to Jesus, but again we have only Christian accounts of this. Prospero the magician is certainly not in competition with Jesus; Shakespeare takes considerable care to exclude Christian references from *The Tempest.* When a chastened Caliban submits to Prospero at the close, his use of the word *grace* initially startles us:

Ay, that I will; and I'll be wise hereafter,
And seek for grace. What a thrice-double ass
Was I, to take this drunkard for a god,
And worship this dull fool!

[V.i.294–97]

Yet what can this mean except that Caliban, having substituted
Stephano for Setebos as his god, now turns to the god Prospero?
It is only after the play ends that the actor who had impersonated
Prospero steps before the curtain to speak in terms that are recog-
nizably Christian, yet are still remote enough from that revelation:

And my ending is despair,
Unless I be reliev'd by prayer,
Which pierces so, that it assaults
Mercy itself, and frees all faults.
    As you from crimes would pardon'd be,
    Let your indulgence set me free.

[Epilogue 15–20]

This is addressed to the audience, whose applause is being so-
licited:

But release me from my bands
With the help of your good hands.

[Epilogue 9–10]

"Indulgence" therefore is audacious wit: the Church pardons,
the audience applauds, and the actor is set free only by approba-
tion of his skill. The role of Prospero, within *The Tempest*'s visionary confines, is godlike; even the magus's angry and impatient
outbursts parody, at a very safe distance, the irascible Yahweh of
the Book of Numbers. *The Tempest* is an elegantly subtle drama

and, like several other Shakespearean masterworks, is hard to hold steady in our view. No audience has ever liked Prospero; Ariel (*pace* the director Wolfe) has a wary affection for the magus, and Miranda loves him, but then he has been both benign mother and stern father to his daughter. Why does Shakespeare make Prospero so cold? The play's ethos does not seem to demand it, and the audience can be baffled by a protagonist so clearly in the right and yet essentially antipathetic. Once the neglectful ruler of Milan, Prospero, successful only as magician and as single parent, goes back to Milan, where evidently he again is not likely to shine as an administrator. Northrop Frye once identified Prospero with Shakespeare, but only in a highly ironic sense, finding in Prospero also:

> a harassed overworked actor-manager, scolding the lazy actors, praising the good ones in connoisseur's language, thinking up jobs for the idle, constantly aware of his limited time before his show goes on, his nerves tense and alert for breakdowns while it is going on, looking forward longingly to peaceful retirement, yet in the meantime having to go out and beg the audience for applause.

That is charming enough to be accurate, and perhaps the harried dramatist-director (he had given up acting, evidently just before writing *Othello*) realized that he himself was becoming colder, no longer the "open and free nature" Ben Jonson praised. There is not much geniality in *The Tempest,* or in other later plays by Shakespeare, except for the role of Autolycus in *The Winter's Tale.* Prospero, as Frye remarks, has no transcendental inclinations, for all his trafficking with spirits. What, besides the revenge he throws aside, could Prospero have been seeking in his Hermetic studies, which in any case began in Milan, long before he had anything to avenge? The Renaissance Hermetist, a Giordano

Bruno or a Dr. John Dee, was seeking knowledge of God, the quest of all gnosis. Not Prospero, for he gives not a single hint that the eternal mysteries spur him on. Unlike Bruno, Prospero the anti-Faust is not a heretic; he is indifferent to the Christian revelation, even as he studies an arcane wisdom that other magi either preferred to Christianity (if, with Bruno, they dared) or more frequently hoped to turn to Christian purposes. Again, we abide in a puzzle: Is Prospero's art, like Shakespeare's, aesthetic rather than mystical? That would make Prospero only the enlargement of a failed metaphor, and belie our experience of the play. Though he stages revels, to his own discomfiture, Prospero is not Ben Jonson, nor Shakespeare.

Evidently, Prospero is a true scholar, pursuing wisdom for its own sake, and yet that rarely could be a dramatic activity, and Prospero is a very successful dramatic representation. But of what? His quest is intellectual, we might even say scientific, though his science is as personal and idiosyncratic as Dr. Freud's. Freud, speaking to his disciples, liked to call himself a conquistador, which seems to me a suggestive epithet for Prospero. Like Freud, Prospero really is the favored one: he is bound to win. Freud's triumph has proved equivocal; much of it expires with the twentieth century. Prospero exults as he approaches his total victory, and then he becomes very sad. No one else in Shakespeare is nearly as successful, except King Henry V. Ironical reversal for Falstaff's bad son takes place only in history, just outside the confines of his play, and in *Henry VI,* where the young Shakespeare opens with Henry V's funeral, French uprisings against the English, and forebodings of civil war in England.

Prospero does not wait for his re-entry into history; ironic loss is all but immediate, even as his forgiven enemies—Caliban included—acknowledge his supremacy, both temporal and mystical. The dynastic marriage of Miranda to the Prince of Naples will unite the two realms and thus prevent further political troubles from outside. But what occult powers, if any, does Prospero still possess after he breaks the staff and drowns his book? I think the singular "book" is meant to contrast with Marlowe's Faustus crying out, "I'll burn my books" when Mephistopheles and the other devils carry him off forever. Faustus has only his library, of Cornelius Agrippa and all the others, but Prospero has "my book," which he has written, the crown of his long labors in reading, brooding, and practicing the control of spirits. That clears away part of the puzzle, and vastly increases the poignance when this conquistador drowns his life's work. It is as though an unpublished Freud threw what would have been the Standard Edition into the sea of space and time.

If there is an analogue between Shakespeare and Prospero, it would have to be their mutual eminence, first among poet-playwrights and supreme among white magicians, or Hermetists. Ben Jonson collected his own works, plays included, and published them in 1616, the year of Shakespeare's death. It was not until 1623 that Shakespeare's friends and coworkers brought out his book, the First Folio, which printed eighteen plays for the first time, with *The Tempest* in pride of place, and with a less jealous Ben Jonson proudly assisting in the enterprise, which after all confirmed his refusal to drown his own book. Prospero does perform that suicidal act, one that needs to be clarified if we are to see *The Tempest* more for what it is and less for the legendary auras it has accumulated.

3

Ariel is our largest clue to understanding Prospero, though we have no similar aid for apprehending this great sprite, who has very little in common with Puck, despite the assertions of many critics. Barely mentioned in the Bible, Ariel seems to have been selected by Shakespeare not for the irrelevant Hebrew meaning of his name (he is no "lion of god" in the play, but a spirit of the elements fire and air), but probably for the sound association between Ariel and aireal. Plainly a contrast to Caliban, all earth and water, Ariel comes into the play before Caliban does, and finally is dismissed to his freedom—his last words to Prospero are "Was't well done?" an actor speaking to a director. Ariel's evidently will be endless play, in the air and in the fire. Caliban, despite his current claque, is grumpily re-adopted by a reluctant Prospero—"this thing of darkness I / Acknowledge mine"—and will go off with his foster father (not his slave owner) to Milan to continue his interrupted education. That seems a visionary prospect indeed, but should cause no more shudders than the future of many Shakespearean marriages: Beatrice and Benedick flailing at each other in late middle age is not a happy vista. Ariel's future, in his terms, is a very cheerful one, though it is beyond Shakespeare's understanding, or ours. Shelley associated Ariel with the freedom of Romantic poetic imagination, which is not altogether un-Shakespearean, but which also is now out of fashion. Whatever happens in *The Tempest* is the work of Ariel, under Prospero's direction, yet it is not solitary labor, as presented upon our stages. The sprite is the leader of a band of angels: "to thy strong bidding task / Ariel and all his quality," they being his subordinates and airy spirits like himself. They, too, presumably are working for their freedom, and are not happy about it, if we can believe Caliban.

Ariel and Prospero play an odd comic turn (wonderfully parodied by Beckett's Clov and Hamm in *Endgame*) in which Ariel's anxiety about the terms of his release from hermetic service and Prospero's uncertain temper combine to keep the audience a little on edge, waiting for an explosion that does not take place (except upon politically correct stages). Frank Kermode usefully reminds us that *The Tempest* "is unquestionably the most sophisticated comedy of a poet whose work in comedy is misunderstood to a quite astonishing degree." It was difficult, surely, to surpass *Twelfth Night, Measure for Measure,* and *The Winter's Tale* in sophistication, yet Shakespeare managed this so brilliantly that, as Kermode implies, we still cannot apprehend fully the comic achievement. I have only rarely heard anyone laugh at a performance of *The Tempest,* but that is because of the directors, whose moral sensibilities never seem to get beyond their politics. The Prospero–Ariel relationship is delicious comedy, together with much else in the play, as I hope to show. What is not at all comic is the mutual torment of the Prospero–Caliban failed adoption, which I will examine again as I turn to a closer consideration of *The Tempest.*

4

The deliberate absence of images in *The Tempest* may have prompted Auden to call his "commentary" *The Sea and the Mirror.* Auden's Prospero says to Ariel that he surrenders his Hermetic library "To the silent dissolution of the sea / Which misuses nothing because it values nothing." Stating with the storm at sea, and ending with Prospero's promise of "calm seas, auspicious gales," *The Tempest* allows us to be washed free of images, one of the comedy's many gifts. We are Miranda, who is adjured to "Sit still, and hear the last of our sea-sorrow." If the sea values nothing, and swallows all, it also keeps nothing, and casts us back again. Ariel's best and most famous song makes our drowned bones into coral, and translates what Hart Crane calls our "lost morning eyes" into pearls.

Ariel suggests a more radical metamorphosis than anyone in the drama actually undergoes. No one fades away, and yet no particular character, not even Prospero, suffers "a sea-change / Into something rich and strange." Perhaps only the complete work of Shakespeare taken as a whole could sustain that metaphor. I wonder again if *The Tempest* was one of Shakespeare's throwaway titles, another "as you like it," or "what you will." The storm is Ariel's creation (the will being Prospero's), and what matters is that it is a sea fiction, a drenching that at last leaves everyone dry. No one is harmed in the play, and forgiveness is extended to all by Prospero, in response to Ariel's most human moment. Everything dissolves in *The Tempest,* except the sea. From one perspective, the sea is dissolution itself, but evidently not so in this unique play. There is no Imogen or Autolycus in *The Tempest*; personality seems no longer to be a prime Shakespearean concern, and is inapplicable anyway to the nonhuman Ariel and half-human Caliban. A visionary comedy was not a new genre for Shakespeare; *A Midsummer Night's Dream* is Bottom's play, yet also Puck's. Still, *The Tempest*—unlike *Cymbeline* and *The Winter's Tale*—is not at all a recapitulation. Mysteriously, it seems an inaugural work, a different mode of comedy, one that Beckett attempted to rival in *Endgame,* a blending of *Hamlet* with *The Tempest*.

Allegory was not a Shakespearean mode, and I find little in *The Tempest*. W.B.C. Watkins, an admirable critic, noted Spenserian elements in Ariel's harpy scene and in the masque of Ceres, neither of which is one of the glories of the play. *The Tempest* provokes speculation, partly because we expect esoteric wisdom from Prospero, though we never receive any. His awesome art is absurdly out of proportion to his purposes; his adversaries are a sorry lot, and could be defeated by a mere Sycorax, rather than by the mightiest of magi. I suspect that anti-Faustianism is again the best clue to Prospero; magic scarcely bears dramatic representation, unless a deflationary element is also at work. Shakespeare was interested in everything, and yet cared far more about inwardness than about magic. When his own so potent art turned aside from inwardness, after the extraordinary fourteen months in which he composed *King Lear, Macbeth,* and *Antony and Cleopatra,* a kind of emptying-out of the self pervaded *Coriolanus* and *Timon of Athens.* The apparent influx of myth and miracle that scholars celebrate in the last plays is more ironic and even farcical than we have taken it to be. Prospero's magic is not always a persuasive substitute for the waning inwardness, and Shakespeare gives signs that he is cognizant of this trouble.

Prospero is nearly as nervous about missed cues and temporal limitations as Macbeth was, and his absolute magic is jumpily aware that its sway cannot be eternal, that its authority is provisional. Authority seems to me the play's mysterious preoccupation. I say "mysterious" because Prospero's authority is unlike anyone else's in Shakespeare. To say what it is not is easy enough: not legal power, even though Prospero was legitimate Duke of Milan. Nor is it precisely moral: Prospero is not truly anxious to justify himself. Perhaps it has a link to what Kent implies when, in the disguise of Caius, he again seeks service with his master, Lear, but Prospero does not have much in him of Lear's divine majesty. Prospero seeks a kind of secularized spiritual authority, and he finally attains something like it, though at considerable human expense to himself. Gerald Hammond, in his wonderful study of seventeenth-century English poetry and poems, *Fleeting Things* (1990), makes a fine observation on how even the opening scene introduces the problem of authority: "*The Tempest* begins its exploration of the uses and abuses of authority with a foundering ship on which passengers and crew are at odds." The honest old Gonzalo admonishes the forthright Boatswain to remember whom he has aboard, and receives a wonderful reply:

> None that I more love than myself. You are a counsellor;
> if you can command these elements to silence, and work
> the peace of the presence, we will not hand a rope more;

use your authority: if you cannot, give thanks you have
lived so long, and make yourself ready in your cabin for the
mischance of the hour, if it so hap. Cheerly, good hearts!
Out of our way, I say.

[I.i.20–27]

The ironic authority has been usurped by Prospero, who
commanded these elements to storm. When we first encounter
Prospero, in the next scene, we hear him urging Miranda to "be
collected" and cease to be distracted by tempest and shipwreck,
since he assures us that no one has been hurt in the slightest. This
is so endlessly suggestive that an audience has to be somewhat
bewildered. If the overwhelming storm—which totally con-
vinced the experienced Boatswain of its menace—is unreal, then
what in the play can be accepted when it appears? A. D. Nuttall
describes much of *The Tempest* as "pre-allegorical," a phenome-
nal sheen that encourages us both to marvel and to be skeptical.
Prospero, though he later seems to be influenced by Ariel's concern for the victims of the mage's illusions, would seem to have
decided upon "the rarer action" of forgiving his enemies even
before he plots to get them under his control.

Since Prospero, through Ariel and his lesser daemons, controls
nature on, and near, the island, the audience never can be sure
what it is that they behold. When Prospero tells us that "bountiful Fortune" has brought his enemies to his shore, we can only
wonder at the cosmological intelligence service that is at play.
Ariel's first entrance (in advance of Caliban's) dissolves no ambi-
guities. This all-powerful spirit had been imprisoned in a pine
tree by the witch Sycorax, and would be there still had not Prospero's Art liberated him. Evidently Ariel has not the resources to
fend off magic, which is thus assigned a potency greater than that
of the angelic world. Fire and air, like Caliban's earth and water,
yield to the Fifth Element of hermetic sages and North African

witches. The pleasantly teasing relationship between Prospero and Ariel contrasts with the fury of hatred between Prospero and Caliban, and yet Ariel, no more than Caliban, has the freedom to evade Prospero's will. Before Act I closes, that potent will charms Prince Ferdinand into a frozen stasis, demonstrating that the human, like the supernatural and the preternatural, is subject to Prospero's Art.

5

We hardly recognize that *The Tempest* is a comedy whenever Prospero is on stage. That may be only a consequence of our acting and directing traditions, which have failed to exploit the contrasts between the anti-Faust's authority and the antics of his hapless enemies. Since Prospero makes no appearance in Act II, the delicious humor comes through, even in some of our current ideological jamborees that pass for productions of *The Tempest*. Shakespeare is subtly genial and shrewd in the dialogues given to his castaways:

> *Adr.* Though this island seem to be desert,—
> *Ant.* Ha, ha, ha!
> *Seb.* So: you're paid.
> *Adr.* Uninhabitable, and almost inaccessible,—
> *Seb.* Yet,—
> *Adr.* Yet,—
> *Ant.* He could not miss't.
> *Adr.* It must needs be of subtle, tender and delicate temperance.
> *Ant.* Temperance was a delicate wench.
> *Seb.* Ay, and a subtle; as he most learnedly deliver'd.
> *Adr.* The air breathes upon us here most sweetly.

Seb. As if it had lungs, and rotten ones.

Ant. Or as 'twere perfumed by a fen.

Gon. Here is everything advantageous to life.

Ant. True; save means to live.

Seb. Of that there's none, or little.

Gon. How lush and lusty the grass looks! how green!

Ant. The ground, indeed, is tawny.

Seb. With an eye of green in 't.

Ant. He misses not much.

Seb. No; he doth but mistake the truth totally.

[II.i.34–55]

Partly, this works as an intricate allusion to the prophet Isaiah's vision of the destruction of Babylon:

Come downe and sit in the dust: a virgine, daughter Babel, sit on the grounde: there is no throne, O daughter of the Chaldeans: for thou shalt no more be called, Tendre and delicate.

[Geneva Bible, Isaiah 47:1]

Temperance, a woman's name among the Puritans, meaning both "calm" and "chaste," is also a word for a moderate climate. Antonio, Prospero's usurping brother, and Sebastian, would-be usurper of his brother, Alonso, King of Naples, are the unredeemable villains of the play. Gonzalo and Adrian, more amiable, are the butts of this nasty duo, but the jokes, on their deeper level, go against the scoffers, since the Isaiah allusion is a warning of the fall that awaits evildoers. The immediate comedy is that Gonzalo and Adrian have the truer perspective, since the isle (though they cannot know this) is enchanted, while Antonio and Sebastian are savage reductionists, who themselves "mistake the truth totally." The audience perhaps begins to understand that perspective governs everything on Prospero's island, which can be seen either as desert or as paradise, depending upon the viewer.

Isaiah and Montaigne fuse in Gonzalo's subsequent rhapsody of an ideal commonwealth that he would establish upon the isle, were he king of it. The taunts of Sebastian and Antonio at this charming prospect prepare us for their attempt to murder the sleeping Alonso and Gonzalo, who are saved by Ariel's intervention, an episode more melodramatic than the comic contest allows us to apprehend seriously. Comedy returns in the meeting between Caliban and King Alonso's jester, Trinculo, and his perpetually intoxicated brother, Stephano. Poor Caliban, hero of our current discourses on colonialism, celebrates his new freedom from Prospero by worshiping Trinculo as his god:

> No more dams I'll make for fish
>> Nor fetch in firing
>> At requiring;
> Nor scrape trenchering, nor wash dish:
>> 'Ban, 'Ban, Cacaliban
> Has a new master:—get a new man.
>
> Freedom, high-day! high-day, freedom! freedom,
> high-day, freedom!

The complexities of Caliban multiply in Act III, where his timid brutality and hatred of Prospero combine in a murderous scheme:

> Why, as I told thee, 'tis a custom with him
> I' th' afternoon to sleep: there thou mayst brain him,
> Having first seiz'd his books; or with a log
> Batter his skull, or paunch him with a stake,
> Or cut his wezand with thy knife. Remember

First to possess his books; for without them
He's but a sot, as I am, nor hath not
One spirit to command: they all do hate him
As rootedly as I. Burn but his books.

[III.ii.85–93]

The viciousness of this contrasts with the aesthetic poignance of Caliban's reaction to the invisible Ariel's music:

Be not afeard; the isle is full of noises,
Sounds and sweet airs, that give delight and hurt not.
Sometimes a thousand twangling instruments
Will hum about mine ears; and sometimes voices,
That, if I then had wak'd after long sleep,
Will make me sleep again: and then, in dreaming,
The clouds methought would open, and show riches
Ready to drop upon me; that, when I wak'd,
I cried to dream again.

[III.ii.133–41]

What reconciles the two passages is Caliban's childishness; he is still very young, and his uncompleted education yielded to the trauma of failed adoption. Shakespeare, inventing the half-human in Caliban, astonishingly blends together the childish and the childlike. As audience, we are repelled by the childish, gruesome fantasies of battering Prospero's skull, or paunching him with a stake, or cutting his windpipe with a knife. Yet only a few moments on, we are immensely moved by the exquisite, childlike pathos of Caliban's Dickensian dream. Far from the heroic rebel that our academic and theatrical ideologues now desire him to become, Caliban is a Shakespearean representation of the family romance at its most desperate, with an authentic changeling who cannot bear his outcast condition.

As a victim of that condition, Caliban is the ironic forerunner of the state of traumatized confusion that Prospero and Ariel will impose upon all of the castaway princes and nobles. Hounded by Ariel in the guise of a Harpy, they at last are herded into a grove near Prospero's cell, to await his judgment. First, the magus celebrates the betrothal of Miranda and Ferdinand with a visionary masque performed by spirits at his command. Poetically, this entertainment seems to me the nadir of *The Tempest,* and I suggest it may be, in some places, a deliberate parody of the court masques that Jonson was composing for James I at the moment that Shakespeare's play was written. Far more important than the masque itself is the manner of its disruption, when Prospero suddenly suffers the crucial trial of his Art. He starts suddenly, and when he speaks, the masque vanishes:

> I had forgot that foul conspiracy
> Of the beast Caliban and his confederates
> Against my life: the minute of their plot
> Is almost come.

> [IV.i.139–42]

Few theatrical coups, even in Shakespeare, match this. On edge throughout the play to seize the propitious moment, Prospero has so lulled himself with the showman's aspect of his Art that he, and all his, nearly are undone. Critics tend to slight Prospero's perturbation here, question its necessity, as if they were so many Ferdinands, finding it "strange." Miranda refutes them when she observes that "Never till this day / Saw I him touch'd with anger, so distemper'd." His anger is not just with "the beast Caliban," discarded foster son, but with himself for failing in alertness, in the control of consciousness. A lifetime of devotion to the strict discipline of Hermetic lore has only barely prevailed, and something in Prospero's self-confidence is forever altered.

I am not at all clear as to why critics should find this a mystery: Shakespeare invents the psychology of overpreparing the event, from which the majority of us suffer. I think of Browning's Childe Roland, one of Shakespeare's heirs, who suddenly comes upon the Dark Tower and chides himself: "Dunce, / Dotard, a-dozing at the very nonce, / After a life spent training for the sight!" Prospero's mastery depends upon a strictly trained consciousness, which must be unrelenting. His momentary letting-go is more than a danger signal and provides his most memorable utterance, addressed to Ferdinand, his prospective son-in-law, and so heir both to Naples and to Milan:

> You do look, my son, in a mov'd sort,
> As if you were dismay'd: be cheerful, sir.
> Our revels now are ended. These our actors,
> As I foretold you, were all spirits, and
> Are melted into air, into thin air:
> And, like the baseless fabric of this vision,
> The cloud-capp'd towers, the gorgeous palaces,
> The solemn temples, the great globe itself,
> Yea, all which it inherit, shall dissolve,
> And, like this insubstantial pageant faded,
> Leave not a rack behind. We are such stuff
> As dreams are made on; and our little life
> Is rounded with a sleep. Sir, I am vex'd;
> Bear with my weakness; my old brain is troubled:
> Be not disturb'd with my infirmity:
> If you be pleas'd, retire into my cell,
> And there repose: a turn or two I'll walk,
> To still my beating mind.

[IV.i.146–63]

A tradition of interpretation, now little credited, read this as Shakespeare's overt farewell to his art. That is certainly rather too reductive, yet one wonders at "the great globe itself," which may contain an ironic reference to Shakespeare's own theater. Whether or not there is a personal element here, Prospero's great declaration confirms the audience's sense that this is a magus without transcendental beliefs, whether Christian or Hermetic–Neo-Platonic. Prospero's vision and the London of towers, palaces, and the Globe itself shall dissolve, not to be replaced by God, heaven, or any other entity. Nor do we appear to have any resurrection: "our little life / Is rounded with a sleep." What the audience sees upon the stage is insubstantial, and so is the audience itself. What vexes Prospero indeed is his infirmity, his lapse of attention, and the murderousness of Caliban, but what might vex the audience is the final realization that this powerful wizard pragmatically is a nihilist, a kind of benign Iago (an outrageous phrase!), whose project of necessity must end in his despair. When he urgently summons Ariel, and says, "Spirit, / We must prepare to meet with Caliban," the telling reply is:

Ay, my commander: when I presented Ceres,
I thought to have told thee of it; but I fear'd
Lest I might anger thee.

[IV.i.167–69]

Since Ariel and Prospero rather easily drive out Caliban, Stephano, and Trinculo, who flee before spirit hounds, we are left to wonder what Ariel might have done had Prospero not roused himself. Not once in the play does Ariel act without a specific order from Prospero, so perhaps the danger from Caliban's plot was more real than many critics concede. There is a certain air of relief in Prospero's language as he addresses Ariel to open Act V, when the culmination is at hand:

Now does my project gather to a head:
My charms crack not; my spirits obey; and time
Goes upright with his carriage. How's the day?

[V.i.1–3]

After ordering Ariel to release the King of Naples and the other worthies, Prospero achieves the zenith of his anti-Faustianism in a great speech of renunciation, which nevertheless provides more fresh queries than answers:

Ye elves of hills, brooks, standing lakes, and groves;
And ye that on the sands with printless foot
Do chase the ebbing Neptune, and do fly him
When he comes back; you demi-puppets that
By moonshine do the green sour ringlets make,
Whereof the ewe not bites; and you whose pastime
Is to make midnight mushrooms, that rejoice
To hear the solemn curfew; by whose aid—
Weak masters though ye be—I have bedimm'd
The noontide sun, call'd forth the mutinous winds,
And 'twixt the green sea and the azur'd vault
Set roaring war: to the dread rattling thunder
Have I given fire, and rifted Jove's stout oak
With his own bolt; the strong-bas'd promontory
Have I made shake, and by the spurs pluck'd up
The pine and cedar: graves at my command
Have wak'd their sleepers, op'd, and let 'em forth
By my so potent Art. But this rough magic
I here abjure; and, when I have requir'd
Some heavenly music—which even now I do,—
To work mine end upon their senses, that
This airy charm is for, I'll break my staff,
Bury it certain fathoms in the earth,

And deeper than did ever plummet sound
I'll drown my book.

[V.i.33–57]

The poetic strength of *The Tempest,* perhaps even of Shake-speare, touches a limit of art in this apparent *kenosis,* or emptying-out, of Prospero's mortal godhood. If I say "apparent," it is because the unholy powers of the magus surpass anything we could have expected, and we wonder if this declaration really can undo his acquired nature, which itself is art. The spirits suppos-edly being dismissed are deprecated as "weak masters," and we have to ask when and why Prospero roused the dead. That art indeed would have been so much more than potent that to term it "rough magic" is altogether inadequate. Which book will be drowned, out of the number in Prospero's library, or is this not his own manuscript?

Prospero's abjuration sounds more like a great assertion of power than like a withdrawal from efficacy. Nothing Prospero says severs him more from Shakespeare than this speech. We are listening not to a poet playwright but to an uncanny magician whose art has become so internalized that it cannot be aban-doned, even though he insists it will be. The single scene that is Act V will continue for some 250 lines, during which Prospero's authority suffers no diminishment. Why do Antonio and Sebast-ian, who express no repentance whatsoever, take no action against Prospero, if he no longer commands spirits? When Pros-pero, in an aside to Sebastian and Antonio, says that he knows of their plot against King Alonso, yet "at this time / I will tell no tales," why do they not cut him down? Sebastian only mutters, in an aside, "The devil speaks in him," and indeed from the per-spective of the villains, the devil does inhabit Prospero, who ter-rifies them. Prospero may yet attempt to abandon his art, but it is not at all clear that his supernatural authority ever will abandon him. His deep melancholy as the play closes may not be related to his supposed renunciation.

Most of what we hear in the remainder of *The Tempest* is triumph, restoration, some reconciliation, and even some hints that Prospero and Caliban will work out their dreadful relationship, but much also is left as puzzle. We are not told that Caliban will be allowed to stay on the island; will he accompany Prospero "to my Milan, where / Every third thought shall be my grave"? The thought of Caliban in Italy is well-nigh unthinkable; what is scarcely thinkable is Antonio in Milan, and Sebastian in Naples. Presumably the marriage of Ferdinand and Miranda will ensure both Naples and Milan against usurpers, though who can say? In some respects, Prospero in Milan as restored ruler is as unsettling a prospect as Caliban continuing his education in that city. Gonzalo, in a remarkable speech, tells us that Ferdinand:

> found a wife
> Where he himself was lost, Prospero his dukedom
> In a poor isle, and all of us ourselves
> When no man was his own.
>
> [V.i.210–13]

Gonzalo encompasses more than he intends, for Prospero's true dukedom may always be that poor isle, where "no man was his own," since all were Prospero's, and only he was his own. How can the magus, whatever his remaining powers may be, find himself his own in Milan?

william shakespeare
the tempest

synopsis

Prospero, Duke of Milan, had been a ruler who preferred a life of studious penetration into Nature's secrets to one of state business and diplomacy. He had placed the entire management of ducal affairs in the hands of his brother Antonio, but this false, ambitious man, with the aid of the powerful Alonso, King of Naples, who wished to annex Milan, ousted Prospero from his dukedom. The conspirators did not dare to kill the Prince outright, so he and his three-year-old daughter were spirited away and set adrift in the open sea in a small boat. Death would have been inevitable, had it not been for the humane firmness of Gonzalo, the Counsellor, who stocked the boat with the necessities of life, including also some rich garments and Prospero's books of magic.

They at last reached a desert island with one lone inhabitant, the misshapen monster, Caliban, son of the wicked witch Sycorax. Prospero released the good spirits imprisoned by Sycorax, trained both them and Caliban to obey his will, and devoted himself to the intensive study of magic and the education of his little daughter Miranda.

Twelve years pass, and Miranda is now an utterly unsophisticated girl of peerless beauty. As the play opens, she is watching with compassionate concern a fine large ship off the coast blazing with flames in a sudden tempest. Prospero tells her it is full of human beings like themselves, and assures her of their safety. Putting aside his magic mantle, he relates to her the whole story of his life, and at the end comes the surprising information that all his enemies are in the vessel which his art has apparently wrecked.

Ariel, chief of the spirits, comes to report gleefully that the ship is safe in harbor; the mariners are asleep under the hatches; and the passengers dispersed over the island, with King Alonso and his party vainly seeking for his lost son Ferdinand. Ariel, by singing, guides the young prince to Prospero's cave where he is startled by the appearance of Miranda whom he thinks the island goddess, while she, in turn, thinks this new creature of noble bearing must be divine. Their mutual attraction delights Prospero, but he resolves to test Ferdinand's strength of character and his avowed love for Miranda, first by challenging him sternly as a spy and traitor, then setting him to work as a prisoner piling heavy logs of wood. Miranda begs Ferdinand to rest, but, despite the lovemaking, the young man works steadily, to Prospero's entire satisfaction.

In one part of the island, ever pursued by Ariel, wanders the disconsolate King. Gonzalo advises him to rest, and, under Ariel's influence, they both fall asleep. The King's brother, Sebastian, and Prospero's false brother, Antonio, plot the death of the two sleeping men, but Ariel frustrates their plans by whispering in Gonzalo's ear. Later, with Prospero present, though invisible, Ariel tantalizes the hungry tired group with the sight of a delicious banquet spread before them, then causes the food to vanish and upbraids them for their cruel treatment in former years of Prospero and his infant daughter.

He tells them they are being punished for their past sins, and leaves them almost senseless with fear. Ariel has also been following the movements of the monster Caliban, who hates Prospero for his mastery of the island. He has been discovered by two sailors who escaped from the wreck and found a cask of wine that had been washed ashore. After they are all drunk, they plot to kill Prospero, with Caliban as their guide, and take possession of the island for themselves. Ariel gives his master full information of Caliban's treachery, but Prospero proceeds with the celebration he has planned in honor of the betrothal of Ferdinand and Miranda.

The beautiful pageant is suddenly cut short by Prospero when he recalls Ariel's warnings of the plot against his life. The conspirators are easily routed by spirits in the shapes of dogs and hounds. The penitent King appears, fetched by Ariel, with Prospero's brother and the others. Prospero recalls to them their guilty deeds, then forgives them, first addressing himself to the kindly Gonzalo, and the King promises to restore him to his dukedom. He leads Alonso to a cell where the astonished King sees his son Ferdinand, given up as lost, playing chess with Miranda. Both father and son are overwhelmed with joy, and the King takes great delight in Miranda who is marvelling at these people from the brave new world in which she is going to live. Ariel escorts their ship safely to Naples, where he is given his freedom by Prospero who forsakes forever his magic art.

historical data

For the main thread of the plot of this play no source has been discovered. There is a notable resemblance in some particulars to a German comedy *Die Schöne Sidea* by Jacob Ayrer, but it is more probable that both derived from the same source than that Shakespeare is indebted to the continental author. The story of the storm and "the still vex'd Bermoothes" were undoubtedly taken from the various accounts of the shipwreck of Sir George Somers' "Sea Venture" off the Bermudas, and the subsequent escape to Virginia in 1609–10. The god Setebos is taken from Eden's *History of Travaile* (1577), a translation of Magellan's *Voyage to the South Pole*. Gonzalo's ideal commonwealth (Act II, Scene i) comes from Florio's translation (1603) of Montaigne's *Essays,* and Prospero's speech renouncing magic was probably suggested by a passage in Goldring's translation of Ovid's *Metamorphoses*. The supernatural episodes and most of the names are almost certainly Shakespeare's invention. It has been ingeniously suggested that Caliban is merely an anagram for "cannibal."

The play could not very well have been written prior to 1609, the year of Somers' wreck, and it was performed during the marriage festivities of King James' daughter, Elizabeth, in 1613. Malone stated that the play was in existence in 1611, and, although an entry in the Revels accounts stating that it had been performed at Whitehall on Hallowmass night during that year is known to be a forgery, faith in Malone's accuracy has generally caused scholars to agree to this year as its date of composition. It did not appear in published form until the First Folio.

dramatis personæ

Alonso, *King of Naples.*

Sebastian, *his brother.*

Prospero, *the right Duke of Milan.*

Antonio, *his brother, the usurping Duke of Milan.*

Ferdinand, *son to the King of Naples.*

Gonzalo, *an honest old Counsellor.*

Adrian,
Francisco, } *Lords.*

Caliban, *a savage and deformed Slave.*

Trinculo, *a Jester.*

Stephano, *a drunken Butler.*

Master of a Ship.

Boatswain.

Mariners.

Miranda, *daughter to Prospero.*

Ariel, *an airy Spirit.*

Iris,
Ceres,
Juno, } *Spirits.*
Nymphs,
Reapers,

Other Spirits *attending on Prospero.*

Scene : A ship at sea; an uninhabited island.

act 1

scene 1. [*On a ship at sea: a tempestuous noise of thunder and lightning heard*]

Enter a Ship-Master *and* a Boatswain

Master. Boatswain!

Boatswain. Here, master: what cheer?

Master. Good, speak to the mariners: fall to't, yarely, or we run ourselves aground. Bestir, bestir!

Exit.

Enter Mariners

Boatswain. Heigh, my hearts! cheerly, cheerly, my hearts! Yare, yare! Take in the topsail. Tend to the master's whistle! Blow, till thou burst thy wind, if room enough!

Enter Alonso, Sebastian, Antonio, Ferdinand, Gonzalo, *and others*

Alonso. Good boatswain, have care. Where's the master? Play the men!

Boatswain. I pray now, keep below!

Antonio. Where is the master, boatswain?

Boatswain. Do you not hear him? You mar our labour.
Keep your cabins: you do assist the storm!

Gonzalo. Nay, good, be patient.

Boatswain. When the sea is. Hence! What cares these roarers for
the name of king? To cabin: silence! Trouble us not.

Gonzalo. Good, yet remember whom thou hast aboard.

Boatswain. None that I more love than myself. You are a
counsellor; if you can command these elements to silence,
and work the peace of the present, we will not hand a rope
more. Use your authority: if you cannot, give thanks you
have lived so long and make yourself ready in your cabin for
the mischance of the hour, if it so hap. Cheerly, good hearts!
Out of our way, I say!

Exit.

Gonzalo. I have great comfort from this fellow. methinks he
hath no drowning mark upon him; his complexion is perfect
gallows. Stand fast, good Fate, to his hanging; make the rope
of his destiny our cable, for our own doth little advantage. If
he be not born to be hanged, our case is miserable.

Exeunt.

Re-enter Boatswain

Boatswain. Down with the topmast! Yare! Lower, lower. Bring
her to try with main-course. [*A cry within*] A plague upon
this howling! They are louder than the weather or our office.
Re-enter Sebastian, Antonio, *and* Gonzalo
Yet again! What do you here? Shall we give o'er and drown?
Have you a mind to sink?

Sebastian. A pox o' your throat, you bawling, blasphemous,
incharitable dog!

Boatswain. Work you, then.

Antonio. Hang, cur! hang, you whoreson, insolent noisemaker!
   We are less afraid to be drowned than thou art.

Gonzalo. I'll warrant him for drowning, though the ship were
   no stronger than a nutshell, and as leaky as an unstanched
   wench.

Boatswain. Lay her a-hold, a-hold! Set her two courses; off to sea
   again. Lay her off.

Enter Mariners, *wet*

Mariners. All lost! To prayers, to prayers! All lost!

Boatswain. What, must our mouths be cold?

Gonzalo. The king and prince, at prayers! Let's assist them, for
   our case is as theirs.

Sebastian.   I'm out of patience.

Antonio. We are merely cheated of our lives by drunkards. This
   wide-chopp'd rascal,—would thou mightst lie drowning the
   washing of ten tides!

Gonzalo.   He'll be hang'd yet, though every drop
   of water swear against it and gape at widest to glut him.
[*A confused noise within*] 'Mercy on us!'—
   'We split, we split!'—'Farewell my wife and children!'—
   'Farewell, brother!'—'We split, we split, we split!'

Antonio. Let's all sink with the king.

Sebastian. Let's take leave of him.

Exeunt Antonio *and* Sebastian.

Gonzalo. Now would I give a thousand furlongs of sea for an
   acre of barren ground, long heath, brown furze, any thing.
   The wills above be done! But I would fain die a dry death.

Exeunt.

scene 2. [*The island. Before* Prospero's *cell*]

Enter Prospero *and* Miranda

Miranda. If by your Art, my dearest father, you have
    Put the wild waters in this roar, allay them.
    The sky, it seems, would pour down stinking pitch
    But that the sea, mounting to th' welkin's cheek,
    Dashes the fire out. O, I have suffer'd
    With those that I saw suffer! A brave vessel
    (Who had, no doubt, some noble creature in her)
    Dash'd all to pieces. O, the cry did knock
    Against my very heart! Poor souls, they perish'd!
    Had I been any god of power, I would
    Have sunk the sea within the earth or ere
    It should the good ship so have swallow'd and
    The fraughting souls within her.

Prospero.   Be collected.
    No more amazement: tell your piteous heart
    There's no harm done.

Miranda.   O, woe the day!

Prospero.   No harm.
    I have done nothing but in care of thee,
    Of thee, my dear one, thee my daughter, who
    Art ignorant of what thou art, nought knowing
    Of whence I am, nor that I am more better
    Than Prospero, master of a full poor cell,
    And thy no greater father.

Miranda.   More to know
    Did never meddle with my thoughts.

Prospero.   'Tis time
  I should inform thee farther. Lend thy hand
  And pluck my magic garment from me.—So:

                        Lays down his mantle.

  Lie there, my Art. Wipe thou thine eyes; have comfort.
  The direful spectacle of the wreck, which touch'd
  The very virtue of compassion in thee,
  I have with such provision in mine art
  So safely order'd, that there is no soul,
  No, not so much perdition as an hair,
  Betid to any creature in the vessel
  Which thou heard'st cry, which thou saw'st sink. Sit down;
  For thou must now know farther.

Miranda.   You have often
  Begun to tell me what I am, but stopp'd,
  And left me to a bootless inquisition,
  Concluding 'Stay, not yet.'

Prospero.   The hour's now come;
  The very minute bids thee ope thine ear.
  Obey and be attentive. Canst thou remember
  A time before we came unto this cell?
  I do not think thou canst, for then thou wast not
  Out three years old.

Miranda.   Certainly, sir, I can.

Prospero. By what? By any other house or person?
  Of any thing the image, tell me, that
  Hath kept with thy remembrance.

Miranda.   'Tis far off,
  And rather like a dream than an assurance
  That my remembrance warrants. Had I not
  Four or five women once that tended me?

Prospero. Thou hadst, and more, Miranda. But how is it
   That this lives in thy mind? What seest thou else
   In the dark backward and abysm of time?
   If thou rememb'rest aught ere thou cam'st here,
   How thou cam'st here thou mayst.

Miranda.   But that I do not.

Prospero. Twelve year since, Miranda, twelve year since,
   Thy father was the Duke of Milan and
   A prince of power.

Miranda.   Sir, are not you my father?

Prospero. Thy mother was a piece of virtue, and
   She said thou wast my daughter; and thy father
   Was Duke of Milan, and his only heir
   And princess, no worse issued.

Miranda.   O the heavens!
   What foul play had we, that we came from thence?
   Or blessed was't we did?

Prospero.   Both, both, my girl:
   By foul play, as thou say'st, were we heaved thence,
   But blessedly holp hither.

Miranda.   O, my heart bleeds
   To think o' the teen that I have turn'd you to,
   Which is from my remembrance! Please you, farther.

Prospero. My brother and thy uncle, call'd Antonio—
   I pray thee, mark me, that a brother should
   Be so perfidious!—he whom, next thyself,
   Of all the world I loved, and to him put
   The manage of my state, as at that time
   Through all the signories it was the first,
   And Prospero the prime Duke, being so reputed
   In dignity, and for the liberal arts

Without a parallel; those being all my study,
The government I cast upon my brother
And to my state grew stranger, being transported
And rapt in secret studies. Thy false uncle—
Dost thou attend me?

Miranda.　　　　　　　Sir, most heedfully.

Prospero. Being once perfected how to grant suits,
　How to deny them, who t' advance, and who
　To trash for over-topping, new created
　The creatures that were mine, I say, or changed 'em,
　Or else new form'd 'em; having both the key
　Of officer and office, set all hearts i' the state
　To what tune pleased his ear, that now he was
　The ivy which had hid my princely trunk
　And suck'd my verdure out on't. Thou attend'st not.

Miranda. O, good sir, I do.

Prospero.　　　　　　　I pray thee, mark me.
　I, thus neglecting worldly ends, all dedicated
　To closeness and the bettering of my mind
　With that which, but by being so retired,
　O'er-prized all popular rate, in my false brother
　Awaked an evil nature; and my trust,
　Like a good parent, did beget of him
　A falsehood in its contrary as great
　As my trust was, which had indeed no limit,
　A confidence sans bound. He being thus lorded,
　Not only with what my revenue yielded
　But what my power might else exact, like one
　Who having into truth by telling of it,
　Made such a sinner of his memory,
　To credit his own lie, he did believe
　He was indeed the duke; out o' the substitution

And executing the outward face of royalty,
With all prerogative. Hence his ambition growing,—
Dost thou hear?

Miranda.   Your tale, sir, would cure deafness.

Prospero. To have no screen between this part he play'd
And him he play'd it for, he needs will be
Absolute Milan. Me, poor man, my library
Was dukedom large enough. Of temporal royalties
He thinks me now incapable; confederates,
So dry he was for sway, wi' the King of Naples
To give him annual tribute, do him homage,
Subject his coronet to his crown, and bend
The dukedom yet unbow'd—alas, poor Milan!—
To most ignoble stooping.

Miranda.   O the heavens!

Prospero. Mark his condition and th' event, then tell me
If this might be a brother.

Miranda.   I should sin
To think but nobly of my grandmother:
Good wombs have borne bad sons.

Prospero.   Now the condition.
This King of Naples, being an enemy
To me inveterate, hearkens my brother's suit,
Which was that he, in lieu o' th' premises
Of homage and I know not how much tribute,
Should presently extirpate me and mine
Out of the dukedom and confer fair Milan,
With all the honours, on my brother. Whereon,
A treacherous army levied, one midnight
Fated to the purpose did Antonio open
The gates of Milan, and i' the dead of darkness,

The ministers for the purpose hurried thence
Me and thy crying self.

Miranda.   Alack, for pity!
I, not rememb'ring how I cried out then,
Will cry it o'er again: it is a hint
That wrings mine eyes to't.

Prospero.   Hear a little further,
And then I'll bring thee to the present business
Which now's upon 's, without the which this story
Were most impertinent.

Miranda.   Wherefore did they not
That hour destroy us?

Prospero.   Well demanded, wench:
My tale provokes that question. Dear, they durst not,
So dear the love my people bore me, nor set
A mark so bloody on the business, but
With colours fairer painted their foul ends.
In few, they hurried us aboard a bark,
Bore us some leagues to sea, where they prepared
A rotten carcass of a butt, not rigg'd,
Nor tackle, sail, nor mast; the very rats
Instinctively have quit it. There they hoist us
To cry to th' sea that roar'd to us, to sigh
To the winds, whose pity, sighing back again,
Did us but loving wrong.

Miranda.   Alack, what trouble
Was I then to you!

Prospero.   O, a cherubin
Thou wast that did preserve me. Thou didst smile,
Infused with a fortitude from heaven,
When I have deck'd the sea with drops full salt,

Under my burthen groan'd, which raised in me
An undergoing stomach to bear up
Against what should ensue.

Miranda.   How came we ashore?

Prospero. By Providence divine,
Some food we had, and some fresh water, that
A noble Neapolitan, Gonzalo,
Out of his charity, who being then appointed
Master of this design, did give us, with
Rich garments, linens, stuffs and necessaries,
Which since have steaded much; so of his gentleness,
Knowing I loved my books, he furnish'd me
From mine own library with volumes that
I prize above my dukedom.

Miranda.   Would I might
But ever see that man!

Prospero.   Now I arise:
                                   Resumes his mantle.
Sit still, and hear the last of our sea-sorrow.
Here in this island we arrived, and here
Have I, thy schoolmaster, made thee more profit
Than other princess can that have more time
For vainer hours, and tutors not so careful.

Miranda. Heavens thank you for't! And now I pray you, sir,
For still 'tis beating in my mind, your reason
For raising this sea-storm?

Prospero.   Know thus far forth.
By accident most strange, bountiful Fortune,
Now my dear lady, hath mine enemies
Brought to this shore; and by my prescience
I find my zenith doth depend upon

A most auspicious star, whose influence
If now I court not, but omit, my fortunes
Will ever after droop. Here cease more questions:
Thou art inclined to sleep; 'tis a good dulness,
And give it way. I know thou canst not choose.

Miranda *sleeps*.

Come away, servant, come. I am ready now.
Approach, my Ariel, come.

Enter Ariel

Ariel. All hail, great master! Grave sir, hail! I come
To answer thy best pleasure; be't to fly,
To swim, to dive into the fire, to ride
On the curl'd clouds, to thy strong bidding task
Ariel and all his quality.

Prospero.   Hast thou, spirit,
Perform'd to point the tempest that I bade thee?

Ariel. To every article.
I boarded the king's ship; now on the beak,
Now in the waist, the deck, in every cabin
I flamed amazement. Sometime I'd divide,
And burn in many places; on the topmast,
The yards and bowsprit would I flame distinctly,
Then meet and join. Jove's lightnings, the precursors
O' the dreadful thunder-claps, more momentary
And sight-outrunning were not: the fire and cracks
Of sulphurous roaring the most mighty Neptune
Seem to besiege, and make his bold waves tremble,
Yea, his dread trident shake.

Prospero.   My brave spirit!
Who was so firm, so constant, that this coil
Would not infect his reason?

Ariel.   Not a soul
But felt a fever of the mad, and play'd
Some tricks of desperation. All but mariners
Plunged in the foaming brine and quit the vessel,
Then all afire with me: the king's son, Ferdinand,
With hair up-staring—then like reeds, not hair—
Was the first man that leap'd, cried 'Hell is empty,
And all the devils are here.'

Prospero.   Why, that's my spirit!
But was not this nigh shore?

Ariel.   Close by, my master.

Prospero. But are they, Ariel, safe?

Ariel.   Not a hair perish'd;
On their sustaining garments not a blemish,
But fresher than before: and, as thou badest me,
In troops I have dispersed them 'bout the isle.
The king's son have I landed by himself;
Whom I left cooling of the air with sighs
In an odd angle of the isle, and sitting,
His arms in this sad knot.

Prospero.   Of the king's ship,
The mariners, say how thou hast disposed,
And all the rest o' the fleet.

Ariel.   Safely in harbour
Is the king's ship; in the deep nook, where once
Thou call'dst me up at midnight to fetch dew
From the still-vex'd Bermoothes, there she's hid:
The mariners all under hatches stow'd,
Who, with a charm join'd to their suffer'd labour,
I have left asleep: and for the rest o' the fleet,
Which I dispersed, they all have met again,

And are upon the Mediterranean flote,
Bound sadly home for Naples,
Supposing that they saw the king's ship wreck'd,
And his great person perish.

Prospero.   Ariel, thy charge
Exactly is perform'd: but there's more work.
What is the time o' the day?

Ariel.   Past the mid season.

Prospero. At least two glasses. The time 'twixt six and now
Must by us both be spent most preciously.

Ariel. Is there more toil? Since thou dost give me pains
Let me remember thee what thou hast promised,
Which is not yet perform'd me.

Prospero.   How now? Moody?
What is't thou canst demand?

Ariel.   My liberty.

Prospero. Before the time be out? No more!

Ariel.   I prithee,
Remember I have done thee worthy service;
Told thee no lies, made thee no mistakings, served
Without or grudge or grumblings: thou didst promise
To bate me a full year.

Prospero.   Dost thou forget
From what a torment I did free thee?

Ariel.   No.

Prospero. Thou dost; and think'st it much to tread the ooze
Of the salt deep,
To run upon the sharp wind of the north,
To do me business in the veins o' the earth
When it is baked with frost.

Ariel.   I do not, sir.

Prospero. Thou liest, malignant thing! Hast thou forgot
    The foul witch Sycorax, who with age and envy
    Was grown into a hoop? hast thou forgot her?

Ariel. No, sir.

Prospero.   Thou hast. Where was she born? Speak; tell me.

Ariel. Sir, in Argier.

Prospero.   O, was she so? I must
    Once in a month recount what thou hast been,
    Which thou forget'st. This damn'd witch Sycorax,
    For mischiefs manifold and sorceries terrible
    To enter human hearing, from Argier,
    Thou know'st, was banish'd. For one thing she did
    They would not take her life. Is not this true?

Ariel. Ay, sir.

Prospero. This blue-eyed hag was hither brought with child,
    And here was left by the sailors. Thou, my slave,
    As thou report'st thyself, wast then her servant;
    And, for thou wast a spirit too delicate
    To act her earthy and abhorr'd commands,
    Refusing her grand hests, she did confine thee,
    By help of her more potent ministers,
    And in her most unmitigable rage,
    Into a cloven pine, within which rift
    Imprison'd thou didst painfully remain
    A dozen years; within which space she died,
    And left thee there, where thou didst vent thy groans
    As fast as mill-wheels strike. Then was this island—
    Save for the son that she did litter here,
    A freckled whelp hag-born—not honour'd with
    A human shape.

Ariel.   Yes, Caliban her son.

Prospero. Dull thing, I say so; he, that Caliban,
    Whom now I keep in service. Thou best know'st
    What torment I did find thee in: thy groans
    Did make wolves howl and penetrate the breasts
    Of ever-angry bears. It was a torment
    To lay upon the damn'd, which Sycorax
    Could not again undo. It was mine art,
    When I arrived and heard thee, that made gape
    The pine, and let thee out.

Ariel.   I thank thee, master.

Prospero. If thou more murmur'st, I will rend an oak,
    And peg thee in his knotty entrails till
    Thou hast howl'd away twelve winters.

Ariel.   Pardon, master:
    I will be correspondent to command,
    And do my spiriting gently.

Prospero.   Do so, and after two days
    I will discharge thee.

Ariel.   That's my noble master!
    What shall I do? Say what; what shall I do?

Prospero. Go make thyself like a nymph o' the sea:
    Be subject to no sight but thine and mine, invisible
    To every eyeball else. Go take this shape
    And hither come in't: go, hence with diligence!

                                        Exit Ariel.

    Awake, dear heart, awake! Thou hast slept well.
    Awake!

Miranda. The strangeness of your story put
    Heaviness in me.

Prospero.   Shake it off. Come on,
We'll visit Caliban my slave, who never
Yields us kind answer.

Miranda.   'Tis a villain, sir,
I do not love to look on.

Prospero.   But as 'tis,
We cannot miss him: he does make our fire,
Fetch in our wood, and serves in offices
That profit us. What ho! slave! Caliban!
Thou earth, thou! Speak.

Caliban. [*Within*]   There's wood enough within.

Prospero. Come forth, I say! there's other business for thee:
Come, thou tortoise! When?
Re-enter Ariel *like a water-nymph*
Fine apparition! My quaint Ariel,
Hark in thine ear.

Ariel.   My lord, it shall be done.

                                                        Exit.

Prospero. Thou poisonous slave, got by the devil himself
Upon thy wicked dam, come forth!
                    Enter Caliban

Caliban. As wicked dew as e'er my mother brush'd
With raven's feather from unwholesome fen
Drop on you both! A south-west blow on ye
And blister you all o'er!

Prospero. For this, be sure, tonight thou shalt have cramps,
Side-stitches that shall pen thy breath up; urchins
Shall forth at vast of night that they may work
All exercise on thee; thou shalt be pinch'd
As thick as honeycomb, each pinch more stinging
Than bees that made 'em.

Caliban.   I must eat my dinner.
   This island's mine, by Sycorax my mother,
   Which thou takest from me. When thou cam'st first,
   Thou strok'dst me, and madest much of me; wouldst give me
   Water with berries in't, and teach me how
   To name the bigger light and how the less,
   That burn by day and night. And then I loved thee,
   And show'd thee all the qualities o' th' isle,
   The fresh springs, brine-pits, barren place and fertile.
   Cursed be I that did so! All the charms
   Of Sycorax, toads, beetles, bats, light on you!
   For I am all the subjects that you have,
   Which first was mine own king, and here you sty me
   In this hard rock, whiles you do keep from me
   The rest o' th' island.

Prospero.   Thou most lying slave,
   Whom stripes may move, not kindness! I have used thee,
   Filth as thou art, with human care, and lodged thee
   In mine own cell, till thou didst seek to violate
   The honour of my child.

Caliban. O ho, O ho! Would't had been done!
   Thou didst prevent me; I had peopled else
   This isle with Calibans.

Prospero.   Abhorred slave,
   Which any print of goodness wilt not take,
   Being capable of all ill! I pitied thee,
   Took pains to make thee speak, taught thee each hour
   One thing or other. When thou didst not, savage,
   Know thine own meaning, but wouldst gabble like
   A thing most brutish, I endow'd thy purposes
   With words that made them known. But thy vile race,
   Though thou didst learn, had that in't which good natures

Could not abide to be with; therefore wast thou
Deservedly confined into this rock,
Who hadst deserved more than a prison.

Caliban. You taught me language, and my profit on't
Is, I know how to curse. The red plague rid you
For learning me your language!

Prospero.   Hag-seed, hence!
Fetch us in fuel and be quick, thou'rt best,
To answer other business. Shrug'st thou, malice?
If thou neglect'st, or dost unwillingly
What I command, I'll rack thee with old cramps,
Fill all thy bones with aches, make thee roar,
That beasts shall tremble at thy din.

Caliban.   No, pray thee.
[*Aside*] I must obey: his art is of such power
It would control my dam's god, Setebos,
And make a vassal of him.

Prospero.   So, slave; hence!

                                        Exit Caliban.

> *Re-enter* Ariel, *invisible, playing and*
> *singing;* Ferdinand *following*
>
> *Ariel's Song*
>
> Come unto these yellow sands,
>   And then take hands:
> Curtsied when you have and kiss'd
>   The wild waves whist:
> Foot it featly here and there,
> And sweet sprites the burthen bear.
>   Hark, hark!
>   *Burden dispersedly*. Bow-wow.
>   The watch-dogs bark:
>   Bow-wow.

Ariel. Hark, hark! I hear
The strain of strutting chanticleer
Cry Cock-a-diddle-dow.

Ferdinand. Where should this music be? i'th' air or th' earth?
It sounds no more: and sure it waits upon
Some god o' th' island. Sitting on a bank,
Weeping again the king my father's wreck,
This music crept by me upon the waters,
Allaying both their fury and my passion
With its sweet air: thence I have follow'd it,
Or it hath drawn me rather. But 'tis gone.
No, it begins again.

Ariel *sings*

Full fathom five thy father lies,
Of his bones are coral made;
Those are pearls that were his eyes:
Nothing of him that doth fade,
But doth suffer a sea-change
Into something rich and strange.
Sea-nymphs hourly ring his knell:
Burden: Ding-dong.

Ariel. Hark! now I hear them—Ding-dong, bell.

Ferdinand. The ditty does remember my drown'd father.
This is no mortal business, nor no sound
That the earth owes:—I hear it now above me.

Prospero. [*To* Miranda] The fringed curtains of thine eye advance,
And say what thou seest yond.

Miranda.   What is't? a spirit?
Lord, how it looks about! Believe me, sir,
It carries a brave form. But 'tis a spirit.

Prospero. No, wench, it eats and sleeps and hath such senses
As we have, such. This gallant which thou seest

Was in the wreck, and but he's something stain'd
With grief, that's beauty's canker, thou mightst call him
A goodly person. He hath lost his fellows,
And strays about to find 'em.

Miranda.   I might call him
A thing divine, for nothing natural
I ever saw so noble.

Prospero. [*Aside*]   It goes on, I see,
As my soul prompts it. Spirit, fine spirit! I'll free thee
Within two days for this.

Ferdinand.   Most sure, the goddess
On whom these airs attend! Vouchsafe my prayer
May know if you remain upon this island,
And that you will some good instruction give
How I may bear me here. My prime request,
Which I do last pronounce, is O you wonder!
If you be maid or no?

Miranda.   No wonder, sir,
But certainly a maid.

Ferdinand.   My language! Heavens!
I am the best of them that speak this speech,
Were I but where 'tis spoken.

Prospero.   How? The best?
What wert thou, if the King of Naples heard thee?

Ferdinand. A single thing, as I am now, that wonders
To hear thee speak of Naples. He does hear me,
And that he does I weep. Myself am Naples,
Who with mine eyes, never since at ebb, beheld
The king my father wreck'd.

Miranda.   Alack, for mercy!

Ferdinand. Yes, faith, and all his lords, the Duke of Milan
  And his brave son being twain.

Prospero. [*Aside*]   The Duke of Milan
  And his more braver daughter could control thee,
  If now 'twere fit to do't. At the first sight
  They have changed eyes. Delicate Ariel,
  I'll set thee free for this. [*To Ferdinand*] A word, good sir.
  I fear you have done yourself some wrong: a word.

Miranda. Why speaks my father so ungently? This
  Is the third man that e'er I saw, the first
  That e'er I sigh'd for: pity move my father
  To be inclined my way!

Ferdinand.   O, if a virgin,
  And your affection not gone forth, I'll make you
  The queen of Naples.

Prospero.   Soft, sir! One word more.
  [*Aside*] They are both in either's powers: but this swift business
  I must uneasy make, lest too light winning
  Make the prize light. [*To* Ferdinand] One word more; I
    charge thee
  That thou attend me. Thou dost here usurp
  The name thou owest not and hast put thyself
  Upon this island as a spy, to win it
  From me, the lord on't.

Ferdinand.   No, as I am a man.

Miranda. There's nothing ill can dwell in such a temple.
  If the ill spirit have so fair a house,
  Good things will strive to dwell with't.

Prospero.   Follow me.
  Speak not you for him; he's a traitor. Come,

I'll manacle thy neck and feet together;
Sea-water shalt thou drink; thy food shall be
The fresh-brook muscles, wither'd roots, and husks
Wherein the acorn cradled. Follow.

Ferdinand.   No,
  I will resist such entertainment till
  Mine enemy has more power.

               Draws, and is charmed from moving.

Miranda.   O dear father,
  Make not too rash a trial of him, for
  He's gentle, and not fearful.

Prospero.   What, I say,
  My foot my tutor? Put thy sword up, traitor,
  Who makest a show but darest not strike, thy conscience
  Is so possess'd with guilt. Come from thy ward,
  For I can here disarm thee with this stick
  And make thy weapon drop.

Miranda.   Beseech you, father.

Prospero. Hence! Hang not on my garments.

Miranda.   Sir, have pity;
  I'll be his surety.

Prospero.   Silence! One word more
  Shall make me chide thee, if not hate thee. What!
  An advocate for an impostor! Hush!
  Thou think'st there is no more such shapes as he,
  Having seen but him and Caliban: foolish wench!
  To the most of men this is a Caliban,
  And they to him are angels.

Miranda.   My affections
  Are, then, most humble. I have no ambition
  To see a goodlier man.

Prospero.　　　　　　　Come on, obey:
　　Thy nerves are in their infancy again,
　　And have no vigour in them.

Ferdinand.　　　　　　　So they are:
　　My spirits, as in a dream, are all bound up.
　　My father's loss, the weakness which I feel,
　　The wreck of all my friends, nor this man's threats,
　　To whom I am subdued, are but light to me,
　　Might I but through my prison once a day
　　Behold this maid. All corners else o' th' earth
　　Let liberty make use of; space enough
　　Have I in such a prison.

Prospero.　　　　　[*Aside*] It works. [*To* Ferdinand] Come on.
　　Thou hast done well, fine Ariel! [*To* Ferdinand] Follow me.
　　[*To* Ariel] Hark what thou else shalt do me.

Miranda.　　　　　　　　　Be of comfort;
　　My father's of a better nature, sir,
　　Than he appears by speech. This is unwonted
　　Which now came from him.

Prospero.　　　　　　　Thou shalt be as free
　　As mountain winds: but then exactly do
　　All points of my command.

Ariel.　　　　　　　To the syllable.

Prospero. Come, follow. Speak not for him.

　　　　　　　　　　　　　　Exeunt.

act 2

scene 1. [*Another part of the island*]

Enter Alonso, Sebastian, Antonio, Gonzalo, Adrian,
Francisco, *and others*

Gonzalo. Beseech you, sir, be merry. You have cause,
So have we all, of joy, for our escape
Is much beyond our loss. Our hint of woe
Is common; every day, some sailor's wife,
The masters of some merchant, and the merchant,
Have just our theme of woe. But for the miracle,
I mean our preservation, few in millions
Can speak like us. Then wisely, good sir, weigh
Our sorrow with our comfort.

Alonso.   Prithee, peace.

Sebastian. He receives comfort like cold porridge.

Antonio. The visitor will not give him o'er so.

Sebastian. Look, he's winding up the watch of his wit; by and by
it will strike.

Gonzalo. Sir—

Sebastian. One: tell.

Gonzalo. When every grief is entertain'd that's offer'd,
  Comes to the entertainer—

Sebastian. A dollar.

Gonzalo. Dolour comes to him, indeed: you have spoken truer
  than you purposed.

Sebastian. You have taken it wiselier than I meant you should.

Gonzalo. Therefore, my lord—

Antonio. Fie, what a spendthrift is he of his tongue!

Alonso. I prithee, spare.

Gonzalo. Well, I have done; but yet,—

Sebastian. He will be talking.

Antonio. Which, of he or Adrian, for a good wager, first begins
  to crow?

Sebastian. The old cock.

Antonio. The cockerel.

Sebastian. Done. The wager?

Antonio. A laughter.

Sebastian. A match!

Adrian. Though this island seem to be desert—

Sebastian. Ha, ha, ha!—So, you're paid.

Adrian. Uninhabitable, and almost inaccessible,—

Sebastian. Yet—

Adrian. Yet—

Antonio. He could not miss't.

Adrian. It must needs be of subtle, tender and delicate temperance.

Antonio. Temperance was a delicate wench.

Sebastian. Ay, and a subtle; as he most learnedly delivered.

Adrian. The air breathes upon us here most sweetly.

Sebastian. As if it had lungs, and rotten ones.

Antonio. Or as 'twere perfumed by a fen.

Gonzalo. Here is everything advantageous to life.

Antonio. True; save means to live.

Sebastian. Of that there's none, or little.

Gonzalo. How lush and lusty the grass looks! How green!

Antonio. The ground, indeed, is tawny.

Sebastian. With an eye of green in't.

Antonio. He misses not much.

Sebastian. No; he doth but mistake the truth totally.

Gonzalo. But the rarity of it is, which is indeed almost beyond credit—

Sebastian. As many vouched rarities are.

Gonzalo. That our garments being, as they were, drenched in the sea, hold, notwithstanding, their freshness and glosses, being rather new-dyed than stained with salt water.

Antonio. If but one of his pockets could speak, would it not say he lies?

Sebastian. Ay, or very falsely pocket up his report.

Gonzalo. Methinks our garments are now as fresh as when we put them on first in Afric, at the marriage of the king's fair daughter Claribel to the King of Tunis.

Sebastian. 'Twas a sweet marriage, and we prosper well in our return.

Adrian. Tunis was never graced before with such a paragon to their queen.

Gonzalo. Not since widow Dido's time.

Antonio. Widow? a pox o' that! How came that widow in? widow Dido!

Sebastian. What if he had said 'widower Æneas' too? Good Lord, how you take it!

Adrian. 'Widow Dido' said you? You make me study of that: she was of Carthage, not of Tunis.

Gonzalo. This Tunis, sir, was Carthage.

Adrian. Carthage?

Gonzalo. I assure you, Carthage.

Antonio. His word is more than the miraculous harp.

Sebastian. He hath raised the wall, and houses too.

Antonio. What impossible matter will he make easy next?

Sebastian. I think he will carry this island home in his pocket, and give it his son for an apple.

Antonio. And sowing the kernels of it in the sea, bring forth more islands.

Gonzalo. I—

Antonio. Why, in good time.

Gonzalo. Sir, were talking that our garments seem now as fresh as when we were at Tunis at the marriage of your daughter, who is now queen.

Antonio. And the rarest that e'er came there.

Sebastian. Bate, I beseech you, widow Dido.

Antonio. O, widow Dido! Ay, widow Dido.

Gonzalo. Is not, sir, my doublet as fresh as the first day I wore it? I mean, in a sort.

Antonio. That sort was well fished for.

Gonzalo. When I wore it at your daughter's marriage.

Alonso. You cram these words into mine ears against
   The stomach of my sense. Would I had never
   Married my daughter there! For coming thence
   My son is lost and, in my rate, she too,
   Who is so far from Italy removed
   I ne'er again shall see her. O thou mine heir
   Of Naples and of Milan, what strange fish
   Hath made his meal on thee?

Francisco.   Sir, he may live.
   I saw him beat the surges under him
   And ride upon their backs. He trod the water,
   Whose enmity he flung aside, and breasted
   The surge most swoln that met him. His bold head
   'Bove the contentious waves he kept, and oar'd
   Himself with his good arms in lusty stroke
   To the shore, that o'er his wave-worn basis bow'd,
   As stooping to relieve him: I not doubt
   He came alive to land.

Alonso.   No, no, he's gone.

Sebastian. Sir, you may thank yourself for this great loss,
   That would not bless our Europe with your daughter,
   But rather loose her to an African,
   Where she, at least, is banish'd from your eye,
   Who hath cause to wet the grief on't.

Alonso.   Prithee, peace.

Sebastian. You were kneel'd to, and importuned otherwise,
   By all of us and the fair soul herself
   Weigh'd between loathness and obedience, at
   Which end o' the beam should bow. We have lost your son,
   I fear, forever: Milan and Naples have

More widows in them of this business' making
Than we bring men to comfort them.
The fault's your own.

Alonso.   So is the dear'st o' the loss.

Gonzalo. My lord Sebastian,
   The truth you speak doth lack some gentleness,
   And time to speak it in. You rub the sore
   When you should bring the plaster.

Sebastian.   Very well.

Antonio. And most chirurgeonly.

Gonzalo. It is foul weather in us all, good sir,
   When you are cloudy.

Sebastian.   Foul weather?

Antonio.   Very foul.

Gonzalo. Had I plantation of this isle, my lord—

Antonio. He'd sow't with nettle-seed.

Sebastian.   Or docks, or mallows.

Gonzalo. And were the king on't, what would I do?

Sebastian. Scape being drunk for want of wine.

Gonzalo. I' the commonwealth I would by contraries
   Execute all things, for no kind of traffic
   Would I admit; no name of magistrate;
   Letters should not be known; riches, poverty,
   And use of service, none; contract, succession,
   Bourn, bound of land, tilth, vineyard, none;
   No use of metal, corn, or wine or oil;
   No occupation; all men idle, all;
   And women too, but innocent and pure;
   No sovereignty—

Sebastian. Yet he would be king on't.

Antonio. The latter end of his commonwealth forgets the beginning.

Gonzalo. All things in common nature should produce
Without sweat or endeavour; treason, felony,
Sword, pike, knife, gun, or need of any engine,
Would I not have; but nature should bring forth
Of it own kind all foison, all abundance,
To feed my innocent people.

Sebastian. No marrying 'mong his subjects?

Antonio. None, man; all idle; whores and knaves.

Gonzalo. I would with such perfection govern, sir,
T' excel the golden age.

Sebastian. 'Save his majesty!

Antonio. Long live Gonzalo!

Gonzalo. And—do you mark me, sir?

Alonso. Prithee, no more: thou dost talk nothing to me.

Gonzalo. I do well believe your highness, and did it to minister occasion to these gentlemen, who are of such sensible and nimble lungs that they always use to laugh at nothing.

Antonio. 'Twas you we laughed at.

Gonzalo. Who in this kind of merry fooling am nothing to you: so you may continue, and laugh at nothing still.

Antonio. What a blow was there given!

Sebastian. An it had not fallen flat-long.

Gonzalo. You are gentlemen of brave mettle. You would lift the moon out of her sphere, if she would continue in it five weeks without changing.

      Enter Ariel *(invisible) playing solemn music*

Sebastian. We would so, and then go a bat-fowling.

Antonio. Nay, good my lord, be not angry.

Gonzalo. No, I warrant you, I will not adventure my discretion
so weakly. Will you laugh me asleep, for I am very heavy?

Antonio. Go sleep, and hear us.

> *All sleep except* Alonso, Sebastian, *and* Antonio.

Alonso. What, all so soon asleep! I wish mine eyes
Would, with themselves, shut up my thoughts: I find
They are inclined to do so.

Sebastian. Please you, sir,
Do not omit the heavy offer of it.
It seldom visits sorrow; when it doth,
It is a comforter.

Antonio. We two, my lord,
Will guard your person while you take your rest,
And watch your safety.

Alonso. Thank you.—Wondrous heavy.

> Alonso *sleeps. Exit* Ariel.

Sebastian. What a strange drowsiness possesses them!

Antonio. It is the quality o' the climate.

Sebastian. Why
Doth it not then our eyelids sink? I find not
Myself disposed to sleep.

Antonio. Nor I. My spirits are nimble.
They fell together all, as by consent;
They dropp'd, as by a thunder-stroke. What might,
Worthy Sebastian?—O, what might?—No more:—
And yet methinks I see it in thy face
What thou shouldst be. The occasion speaks thee, and
My strong imagination sees a crown
Dropping upon thy head.

Sebastian.   What, art thou waking?

Antonio. Do you not hear me speak?

Sebastian.   I do, and surely
   It is a sleepy language, and thou speak'st
   Out of thy sleep. What is it thou didst say?
   This is a strange repose, to be asleep
   With eyes wide open—standing, speaking, moving,
   And yet so fast asleep.

Antonio.   Noble Sebastian,
   Thou let'st thy fortune sleep—die, rather; wink'st
   Whiles thou art waking.

Sebastian.   Thou dost snore distinctly.
   There's meaning in thy snores.

Antonio. I am more serious than my custom. You
   Must be so too, if heed me, which to do
   Trebles thee o'er.

Sebastian.   Well, I am standing water.

Antonio. I'll teach you how to flow.

Sebastian.   Do so: to ebb
   Hereditary sloth instructs me.

Antonio.   O,
   If you but knew how you the purpose cherish
   Whiles thus you mock it! How, in stripping it,
   You more invest it! Ebbing men, indeed,
   Most often do so near the bottom run
   By their own fear or sloth.

Sebastian.   Prithee, say on:
   The setting of thine eye and cheek proclaim
   A matter from thee, and a birth, indeed,
   Which throes thee much to yield.

Antonio.   Thus, sir:
   Although this lord of weak remembrance, this
   Who shall be of as little memory
   When he is earth'd, hath here almost persuaded—
   For he's a spirit of persuasion, only
   Professes to persuade—the king his son's alive,
   'Tis as impossible that he's undrown'd
   As he that sleeps here swims.

Sebastian.   I have no hope
   That he's undrown'd.

Antonio.   O, out of that 'no hope'
   What great hope have you! No hope that way is
   Another way so high a hope that even
   Ambition cannot pierce a wink beyond,
   But doubt discovery there. Will you grant with me
   That Ferdinand is drown'd?

Sebastian.   He's gone.

Antonio.   Then tell me,
   Who's the next heir of Naples?

Sebastian.   Claribel.

Antonio. She that is queen of Tunis; she that dwells
   Ten leagues beyond man's life; she that from Naples
   Can have no note, unless the sun were post—
   The man i' the moon's too slow—till new-born chins
   Be rough and razorable; she that from whom
   We all were sea-swallow'd, though some cast again,
   And by that destiny to perform an act
   Whereof what's past is prologue, what to come
   In yours and my discharge.

Sebastian.   What stuff is this? How say you?
   'Tis true, my brother's daughter's queen of Tunis,

So is she heir of Naples, 'twixt which regions
There is some space.

Antonio.   A space whose every cubit
Seems to cry out, 'How shall that Claribel
Measure us back to Naples? Keep in Tunis,
And let Sebastian wake.' Say this were death
That now hath seized them; why, they were no worse
Than now they are. There be that can rule Naples
As well as he that sleeps; lords that can prate
As amply and unnecessarily
As this Gonzalo; I myself could make
A chough of as deep chat. O, that you bore
The mind that I do! what a sleep were this
For your advancement! Do you understand me?

Sebastian. Methinks I do.

Antonio.   And how does your content
Tender your own good fortune?

Sebastian.   I remember
You did supplant your brother Prospero.

Antonio.   True:
And look how well my garments sit upon me
Much feater than before. My brother's servants
Were then my fellows; now they are my men.

Sebastian. But, for your conscience?

Antonio. Ay, sir, where lies that? if 'twere a kibe,
'Twould put me to my slipper, but I feel not
This deity in my bosom: twenty consciences,
That stand 'twixt me and Milan, candied be they,
And melt, ere they molest! Here lies your brother,
No better than the earth he lies upon.

If he were that which now he's like, that's dead,
Whom I with this obedient steel, three inches of it,
Can lay to bed forever; whiles you, doing thus,
To the perpetual wink for aye might put
This ancient morsel, this Sir Prudence, who
Should not upbraid our course. For all the rest,
They'll take suggestion as a cat laps milk;
They'll tell the clock to any business that
We say befits the hour.

Sebastian.   Thy case, dear friend,
  Shall be my precedent; as thou got'st Milan,
  I'll come by Naples. Draw thy sword: one stroke
  Shall free thee from the tribute which thou payest,
  And I the king shall love thee.

Antonio.   Draw together,
  And when I rear my hand, do you the like
  To fall it on Gonzalo.

Sebastian.   O, but one word.

                                  They talk apart.

                Re-enter Ariel *invisible*

Ariel. My master through his art foresees the danger
  That you, his friend, are in, and sends me forth—
  For else his project dies—to keep them living.
                          Sings in Gonzalo's *ear.*

               While you here do snoring lie,
               Open-eyed conspiracy
                   His time doth take.
               If of life you keep a care,
               Shake off slumber and beware:
                   Awake, awake!

Antonio. Then let us both be sudden.

Gonzalo. [*Wakes*] Now, good angels
   Preserve the king!

                                                    The rest wake.

Alonso. Why, how now? Ho, awake!—why are you drawn?
   Wherefore this ghastly looking?

Gonzalo.   What's the matter?

Sebastian. Whiles we stood here securing your repose,
   Even now, we heard a hollow burst of bellowing
   Like bulls, or rather lions: Did't not wake you?
   It struck mine ear most terribly.

Alonso.   I heard nothing.

Antonio. O, 'twas a din to fright a monster's ear,
   To make an earthquake! Sure it was the roar
   Of a whole herd of lions.

Alonso.   Heard you this, Gonzalo?

Gonzalo. Upon mine honour, sir, I heard a humming,
   And that a strange one too, which did awake me.
   I shaked you, sir, and cried. As mine eyes open'd,
   I saw their weapons drawn:—there was a noise,
   That's verily. 'Tis best we stand upon our guard,
   Or that we quit this place. Let's draw our weapons.

Alonso. Lead off this ground; and let's make further search
   For my poor son.

Gonzalo.   Heavens keep him from these beasts!
   For he is, sure, i' th' island.

Alonso.   Lead away.

Ariel. Prospero my lord shall know what I have done.
   So, king, go safely on to seek thy son.

                                                    Exeunt.

scene 2. [*Another part of the island*]

Enter Caliban *with a burden of wood. A noise of thunder heard.*

Caliban. All the infections that the sun sucks up
From bogs, fens, flats, on Prosper fall, and make him
By inch-meal a disease! His spirits hear me,
And yet I needs must curse. But they'll nor pinch,
Fright me with urchin-shows, pitch me i' the mire,
Nor lead me, like a firebrand, in the dark
Out of my way, unless he bid 'em. But
For every trifle are they set upon me:
Sometime like apes, that mow and chatter at me
And after bite me; then like hedgehogs, which
Lie tumbling in my barefoot way and mount
Their pricks at my footfall. Sometime am I
All wound with adders, who with cloven tongues
Do hiss me into madness.

Enter Trinculo
Lo, now, lo!

Here comes a spirit of his, and to torment me
For bringing wood in slowly. I'll fall flat;
Perchance he will not mind me.

Trinculo. Here's neither bush nor shrub to bear off any weather
at all, and another storm brewing; I hear it sing i' the wind:
yond same black cloud, yond huge one, looks like a foul
bombard that would shed his liquor. If it should thunder as it
did before, I know not where to hide my head: yond same
cloud cannot choose but fall by pailfuls. What have we here?
A man or a fish? Dead or alive? A fish: he smells like a fish; a
very ancient and fish-like smell; a kind of not of the newest
Poor-John. A strange fish! Were I in England now, as once I

was, and had but this fish painted, not a holiday fool there but would give a piece of silver. There would this monster make a man; any strange beast there makes a man. When they will not give a doit to relieve a lame beggar, they will lay out ten to see a dead Indian. Legged like a man! And his fins like arms! Warm, o' my troth! I do now let loose my opinion, hold it no longer: this is no fish, but an islander, that hath lately suffered by a thunderbolt. [*Thunder*] Alas, the storm is come again! My best way is to creep under his gaberdine; there is no other shelter hereabout. Misery acquaints a man with strange bed-fellows. I will here shroud till the dregs of the storm be past.

   Enter Stephano, *singing: a bottle in his hand*

Stephano.   I shall no more to sea, to sea,
         Here shall I die ashore,—

This is a very scurvy tune to sing at a man's funeral: well, here's my comfort.

                 Drinks.

         Sings
  The master, the swabber, the boatswain, and I,
    The gunner, and his mate,
  Loved Mall, Meg, and Marian, and Margery,
    But none of us cared for Kate;
    For she had a tongue with a tang,
    Would cry to a sailor, Go hang!
  She loved not the savour of tar nor of pitch;
  Yet a tailor might scratch her where'er she did itch.
    Then, to sea, boys, and let her go hang!

This is a scurvy tune too: but here's my comfort.

                 Drinks.

Caliban. Do not torment me:—O!

Stephano. What's the matter? Have we devils here? Do you put tricks upon 's with salvages and men of Ind, ha? I have not scaped drowning, to be afeard now of your four legs; for it hath been said, "As proper a man as ever went on four legs cannot make him give ground." And it shall be said so again, while Stephano breathes at nostrils.

Caliban. The spirit torments me:—O!

Stephano. This is some monster of the isle with four legs, who hath got, as I take it, an ague. Where the devil should he learn our language? I will give him some relief, if it be but for that. If I can recover him and keep him tame, and get to Naples with him, he's a present for any emperor that ever trod on neat's-leather.

Caliban. Do not torment me, prithee; I'll bring my wood home faster.

Stephano. He's in his fit now, and does not talk after the wisest. He shall taste of my bottle: if he have never drunk wine afore, it will go near to remove his fit. If I can recover him and keep him tame, I will not take too much for him; he shall pay for him that hath him, and that soundly.

Caliban. Thou dost me yet but little hurt. Thou wilt anon, I know it by thy trembling: now Prosper works upon thee.

Stephano. Come on your ways; open your mouth. Here is that which will give language to you, cat: open your mouth. This will shake your shaking, I can tell you, and that soundly you cannot tell who's your friend. Open your chaps again.

Trinculo. I should know that voice: it should be—but he is drowned, and these are devils:—O defend me!

Stephano. Four legs and two voices—a most delicate monster! His forward voice, now, is to speak well of his friend; his backward voice is to utter foul speeches and to detract. If all the wine in my bottle will recover him, I will help his ague. Come:—Amen! I will pour some in thy other mouth.

Trinculo. Stephano!

Stephano. Doth thy other mouth call me? Mercy, mercy! This is a devil, and no monster. I will leave him; I have no long spoon.

Trinculo. Stephano! If thou beest Stephano, touch me and speak to me, for I am Trinculo—be not afeard—thy good friend Trinculo.

Stephano. If thou beest Trinculo, come forth: I'll pull thee by the lesser legs. If any be Trinculo's legs, these are they. Thou art very Trinculo indeed! How camest thou to be the siege of this moon-calf? Can he vent Trinculos?

Trinculo. I took him to be killed with a thunder-stroke. But art thou not drowned, Stephano? I hope, now, thou art not drowned. Is the storm overblown? I hid me under the dead moon-calf's gaberdine for fear of the storm. And art thou living, Stephano? O Stephano, two Neapolitans 'scaped!

Stephano. Prithee, do not turn me about; my stomach is not constant.

Caliban. [*Aside*] These be fine things, an if they be not sprites. That's a brave god and bears celestial liquor:
I will kneel to him.

Stephano. How didst thou 'scape? How camest thou hither? Swear, by this bottle, how thou camest hither. I escaped upon a butt of sack, which the sailors heaved o'erboard, by this bottle! Which I made of the bark of a tree with mine own hands, since I was cast ashore.

Caliban. I'll swear, upon that bottle, to be thy true subject, for the liquor is not earthly.

Stephano. Here, swear then how thou escapedst.

Trinculo. Swum ashore, man, like a duck: I can swim like a duck, I'll be sworn.

Stephano. Here, kiss the book. Though thou canst swim like a duck, thou art made like a goose.

Trinculo. O Stephano, hast any more of this?

Stephano. The whole butt, man: my cellar is in a rock by the seaside, where my wine is hid. How now, moon-calf! How does thine ague?

Caliban. Hast thou not dropp'd from heaven?

Stephano. Out o' the moon, I do assure thee. I was the man i' the moon when time was.

Caliban. I have seen thee in her, and I do adore thee. My mistress show'd me thee, and thy dog and thy bush.

Stephano. Come, swear to that. Kiss the book. I will furnish it anon with new contents: swear.

Trinculo. By this good light, this is a very shallow monster! I afeard of him? A very weak monster! The man i' the moon! A most poor credulous monster! Well drawn, monster, in good sooth!

Caliban. I'll show thee every fertile inch o' th' island, and I will kiss thy foot. I prithee, be my god.

Trinculo. By this light, a most perfidious and drunken monster! When's god's asleep, he'll rob his bottle.

Caliban. I'll kiss thy foot. I'll swear myself thy subject.

Stephano. Come on, then, down and swear.

Trinculo. I shall laugh myself to death at this puppy-headed monster. A most scurvy monster! I could find in my heart to beat him—

Stephano. Come, kiss.

Trinculo. But that the poor monster's in drink. An abominable monster!

Caliban. I'll show thee the best springs; I'll pluck thee berries;
    I'll fish for thee, and get thee wood enough.
    A plague upon the tyrant that I serve!
    I'll bear him no more sticks, but follow thee,
    Thou wondrous man.

Trinculo. A most ridiculous monster, to make a wonder of a
    poor drunkard!

Caliban. I prithee, let me bring thee where crabs grow,
    And I with my long nails will dig thee pig-nuts;
    Show thee a jay's nest, and instruct thee how
    To snare the nimble marmoset; I'll bring thee
    To clust'ring filberts, and sometimes I'll get thee
    Young scamels from the rock. Wilt thou go with me?

Stephano. I prithee now, lead the way without any more talking.
    Trinculo, the king and all our company else being drowned,
    we will inherit here. Here, bear my bottle: fellow Trinculo,
    we'll fill him by and by again.

Caliban. [*Sings drunkenly*] Farewell, master; farewell, farewell!

Trinculo. A howling monster, a drunken monster!

Caliban.   No more dams I'll make for fish;
        Nor fetch in firing
        At requiring;
     Nor scrape trencher, nor wash dish:
        'Ban, 'Ban, Cacaliban
        Has a new master:—get a new man.

Freedom, high-day! high-day, freedom! freedom, high-day,
    freedom!

Stephano. O brave monster! Lead the way.

                             Exeunt.

act 3

scene 1. [*Before* Prospero's *cell*]

Enter Ferdinand, *bearing a log*

Ferdinand. There be some sports are painful, and their labour
    Delight in them sets off. Some kinds of baseness
    Are nobly undergone, and most poor matters
    Point to rich ends. This my mean task
    Would be as heavy to me as odious, but
    The mistress which I serve quickens what's dead,
    And makes my labours pleasures: O, she is
    Ten times more gentle than her father's crabbed,
    And he's composed of harshness. I must remove
    Some thousands of these logs and pile them up,
    Upon a sore injunction. My sweet mistress
    Weeps when she sees me work and says such baseness
    Had never like executor. I forget:
    But these sweet thoughts do even refresh my labours
    Most busilest, when I do it.

        Enter Miranda, *and* Prospero *at a distance, unseen*

Miranda.   Alas, now, pray you,
Work not so hard. I would the lightning had
Burnt up those logs that you are enjoin'd to pile!
Pray, set it down and rest you. When this burns,
'Twill weep for having wearied you. My father
Is hard at study; pray now, rest yourself.
He's safe for these three hours.

Ferdinand.   O most dear mistress,
The sun will set before I shall discharge
What I must strive to do.

Miranda.   If you'll sit down,
I'll bear your logs the while. Pray give me that;
I'll carry it to the pile.

Ferdinand.   No, precious creature,
I had rather crack my sinews, break my back,
Than you should such dishonour undergo,
While I sit lazy by.

Miranda.   It would become me
As well as it does you, and I should do it
With much more ease, for my good will is to it,
And yours it is against.

Prospero. [*Aside*]   Poor worm, thou art infected!
This visitation shows it.

Miranda.   You look wearily.

Ferdinand. No, noble mistress, 'tis fresh morning with me
When you are by at night. I do beseech you—
Chiefly that I might set it in my prayers—
What is your name?

Miranda.   Miranda.—O my father,
I have broke your hest to say so!

Ferdinand.   Admired Miranda!
  Indeed the top of admiration! Worth
  What's dearest to the world! Full many a lady
  I have eyed with best regard, and many a time
  The harmony of their tongues hath into bondage
  Brought my too diligent ear. For several virtues
  Have I liked several women; never any
  With so full soul, but some defect in her
  Did quarrel with the noblest grace she owed
  And put it to the foil. But you, O you,
  So perfect and so peerless, are created
  Of every creature's best!

Miranda.   I do not know
  One of my sex, no woman's face remember,
  Save, from my glass, mine own. Nor have I seen
  More that I may call men than you, good friend,
  And my dear father. How features are abroad
  I am skilless of, but by my modesty,
  The jewel in my dower, I would not wish
  Any companion in the world but you,
  Nor can imagination form a shape,
  Besides yourself, to like of. But I prattle
  Something too wildly, and my father's precepts
  I therein do forget.

Ferdinand.   I am, in my condition,
  A prince, Miranda; I do think, a king—
  I would not so!—and would no more endure
  This wooden slavery than to suffer
  The flesh-fly blow my mouth. Hear my soul speak:
  The very instant that I saw you did
  My heart fly to your service; there resides,

    To make me slave to it, and for your sake
    Am I this patient log-man.

Miranda.   Do you love me?

Ferdinand. O heaven, O earth, bear witness to this sound,
    And crown what I profess with kind event,
    If I speak true! If hollowly, invert
    What best is boded me to mischief! I,
    Beyond all limit of what else i' the world,
    Do love, prize, honour you.

Miranda.   I am a fool
    To weep at what I am glad of.

Prospero. [*Aside*]   Fair encounter
    Of two most rare affections! Heavens rain grace
    On that which breeds between 'em.

Ferdinand.   Wherefore weep you?

Miranda. At mine unworthiness, that dare not offer
    What I desire to give, and much less take
    What I shall die to want. But this is trifling,
    And all the more it seeks to hide itself,
    The bigger bulk it shows. Hence, bashful cunning!
    And prompt me, plain and holy innocence!
    I am your wife, if you will marry me;
    If not, I'll die your maid. To be your fellow
    You may deny me; but I'll be your servant,
    Whether you will or no.

Ferdinand.   My mistress, dearest,
    And I thus humble ever.

Miranda.   My husband, then?

Ferdinand. Ay, with a heart as willing
    As bondage e'er of freedom: here's my hand.

Miranda. And mine, with my heart in't. And now farewell
   Till half an hour hence.

Ferdinand.   A thousand thousand!

                             Exeunt Ferdinand *and* Miranda.

Prospero. So glad of this as they I cannot be,
   Who are surprised withal, but my rejoicing
   At nothing can be more. I'll to my book,
   For yet, ere supper-time, must I perform
   Much business appertaining.

                                        Exit.

scene 2.   [*Another part of the island*]

Enter Caliban, Stephano, *and* Trinculo

Stephano. Tell not me—when the butt is out, we will drink
   water; not a drop before. Therefore bear up, and board 'em.
   Servant-monster, drink to me.

Trinculo. Servant-monster! The folly of this island! They say
   there's but five upon this isle: we are three of them; if th'
   other two be brained like us, the state totters.

Stephano. Drink, servant-monster, when I bid thee. Thy eyes are
   almost set in thy head.

Trinculo. Where should they be set else? He were a brave
   monster indeed, if they were set in his tail.

Stephano. My man-monster hath drowned his tongue in sack.
   For my part, the sea cannot drown me; I swam, ere I could
   recover the shore, five-and-thirty leagues off and on. By this
   light, thou shalt be my lieutenant, monster, or my standard.

Trinculo. Your lieutenant, if you list; he's no standard.

Stephano. We'll not run, Monsieur Monster.

Trinculo. Nor go neither; but you'll lie like dogs and yet say
nothing neither.

Stephano. Moon-calf, speak once in thy life, if thou beest a good
moon-calf.

Caliban. How does thy honour? Let me lick thy shoe.
I'll not serve him; he is not valiant.

Trinculo. Thou liest, most ignorant monster: I am in case to justle
a constable. Why, thou deboshed fish, thou, was there ever man
a coward that hath drunk so much sack as I today? Wilt thou
tell a monstrous lie, being but half a fish and half a monster?

Caliban. Lo, how he mocks me! Wilt thou let him, my lord?

Trinculo. 'Lord,' quoth he! That a monster should be such a
natural!

Caliban. Lo, lo, again! Bite him to death, I prithee.

Stephano. Trinculo, keep a good tongue in your head: if you
prove a mutineer—the next tree! The poor monster's my
subject, and he shall not suffer indignity.

Caliban. I thank my noble lord. Wilt thou be pleased to hearken
once again to the suit I made to thee?

Stephano. Marry, will I. Kneel and repeat it; I will stand and so
shall Trinculo.

Enter Ariel, *invisible*

Caliban. As I told thee before, I am subject to a tyrant, a
sorcerer, that by his cunning hath cheated me of the island.

Ariel. [*In Trinculo's voice*] Thou liest.

Caliban.   Thou liest, thou jesting monkey, thou.
I would my valiant master would destroy thee!
I do not lie.

Stephano. Trinculo, if you trouble him any more in's tale, by this
hand, I will supplant some of your teeth.

Trinculo. Why, I said nothing.

Stephano. Mum, then, and no more. Proceed.

Caliban. I say, by sorcery he got this isle;
From me he got it. If thy greatness will
Revenge it on him—for I know thou darest,
But this thing dare not—

Stephano. That's most certain.

Caliban. Thou shalt be lord of it, and I'll serve thee.

Stephano. How now shall this be compassed? Canst thou bring
me to the party?

Caliban. Yea, yea, my lord: I'll yield him thee asleep,
Where thou mayst knock a nail into his head.

Ariel. [*In Trinculo's voice*] Thou liest; thou canst not.

Caliban. What a pied ninny's this! Thou scurvy patch!
I do beseech thy greatness, give him blows,
And take his bottle from him. When that's gone,
He shall drink nought but brine, for I'll not show him
Where the quick freshes are.

Stephano. Trinculo, run into no further danger: interrupt the
monster one word further, and, by this hand, I'll turn my
mercy out o' doors, and make a stock-fish of thee.

Trinculo. Why, what did I? I did nothing. I'll go farther off.

Stephano. Didst thou not say he lied?

Ariel. [*In Trinculo's voice*] Thou liest.

Stephano. Do I so? Take thou that. [*Beats him*] As you like this,
give me the lie another time.

Trinculo. I did not give the lie. Out o' your wits, and hearing
too? A pox o' your bottle! This can sack and drinking do. A
murrain on your monster and the devil take your fingers!

Caliban. Ha, ha, ha!

Stephano. Now, forward with your tale—[*To* Trinculo] Prithee, stand farther off.

Caliban. Beat him enough: after a little time, I'll beat him too.

Stephano.   Stand farther—[*To* Caliban] Come, proceed.

Caliban. Why, as I told thee, 'tis a custom with him
I' th' afternoon to sleep. There thou mayst brain him,
Having first seized his books, or with a log
Batter his skull, or paunch him with a stake,
Or cut his wezand with thy knife. Remember
First to possess his books, for without them
He's but a sot, as I am, nor hath not
One spirit to command: they all do hate him
As rootedly as I. Burn but his books.
He has brave utensils—for so he calls them—
Which, when he has a house, he'll deck withal.
And that most deeply to consider is
The beauty of his daughter; he himself
Calls her a nonpareil. I never saw a woman,
But only Sycorax my dam and she;
But she as far surpasseth Sycorax
As great'st does least.

Stephano.   Is it so brave a lass?

Caliban. Ay, lord; she will become thy bed, I warrant,
And bring thee forth brave brood.

Stephano. Monster, I will kill this man. His daughter and I will
be king and queen—save our Graces!—and Trinculo and
thyself shall be viceroys. Dost thou like the plot, Trinculo?

Trinculo. Excellent.

Stephano. Give me thy hand. I am sorry I beat thee, but while
thou livest, keep a good tongue in thy head.

Caliban. Within this half hour will he be asleep.
Wilt thou destroy him then?

Stephano.   Ay, on mine honour.

Ariel. [*Aside*] This will I tell my master.

Caliban. Thou mak'st me merry; I am full of pleasure.
Let us be jocund. Will you troll the catch
You taught me but while-ere?

Stephano. At thy request, monster, I will do reason, any
reason.—Come on, Trinculo, let us sing.

> *Sings*.
> Flout 'em and scout 'em,
> and scout 'em and flout 'em;
> Thought is free.

Caliban. That's not the tune.

> *Ariel plays the tune on a tabor and pipe*.

Stephano. What is this same?

Trinculo. This is the tune of our catch, played by the picture of
Nobody.

Stephano. If thou beest a man, show thyself in thy likeness: if
thou beest a devil, take't as thou list.

Trinculo. O, forgive me my sins!

Stephano. He that dies pays all debts: I defy thee. Mercy upon us!

Caliban. Art thou afeard?

Stephano. No, monster, not I.

Caliban. Be not afeard. The isle is full of noises,
Sounds and sweet airs that give delight, and hurt not.
Sometimes a thousand twangling instruments

Will hum about mine ears; and sometime voices,
That if I then had waked after long sleep,
Will make me sleep again; and then in dreaming,
The clouds methought would open and show riches
Ready to drop upon me, that when I waked,
I cried to dream again.

Stephano. This will prove a brave kingdom to me, where I shall
have my music for nothing.

Caliban. When Prospero is destroyed.

Stephano. That shall be by and by: I remember the story.

Trinculo. The sound is going away. Let's follow it, and after do
our work.

Stephano. Lead, monster, we'll follow. I would I could see this
taborer; he lays it on.

Trinculo. [*To* Caliban] Wilt come? I'll follow, Stephano.

Exeunt.

scene 3.   [*Another part of the island*]

Enter Alonso, Sebastian, Antonio, Gonzalo,
Adrian, Francisco, *and others*

Gonzalo. By'r lakin, I can go no further, sir;
My old bones aches. Here's a maze trod, indeed,
Through forth-rights and meanders! By your patience,
I needs must rest me.

Alonso.   Old lord, I cannot blame thee,
Who am myself attach'd with weariness,
To the dulling of my spirits. Sit down and rest.
Even here I will put off my hope, and keep it
No longer for my flatterer: he is drown'd

Whom thus we stray to find, and the sea mocks
Our frustrate search on land. Well, let him go.

Antonio. [*Aside to* Sebastian] I am right glad that he's so out of
hope.
Do not, for one repulse, forgo the purpose
That you resolved to effect.

Sebastian. [*Aside to* Antonio]   The next advantage
Will we take throughly.

Antonio. [*Aside to* Sebastian] Let it be tonight,
For, now they are oppress'd with travel, they
Will not, nor cannot, use such vigilance
As when they are fresh.

Sebastian. [*Aside to* Antonio] I say, tonight. No more.
                                        Solemn and strange music.

Alonso. What harmony is this?—My good friends, hark!

Gonzalo. Marvellous sweet music!
    Enter Prospero *above, invisible. Enter several strange Shapes,*
    bringing in a banquet: they dance about it with gentle actions of
    salutation; and, inviting the King, &c. to eat, they depart.

Alonso. Give us kind keepers, heavens!—What were these?

Sebastian. A living drollery. Now I will believe
That there are unicorns; that in Arabia
There is one tree, the phoenix' throne, one phoenix
At this hour reigning there.

Antonio.   I'll believe both;
And what does else want credit, come to me
And I'll be sworn 'tis true. Travellers ne'er did lie,
Though fools at home condemn 'em.

Gonzalo.   If in Naples
I should report this now, would they believe me?

If I should say, I saw such islanders—
For certes, these are people of the island—
Who, though they are of monstrous shape, yet note,
Their manners are more gentle-kind than of
Our human generation you shall find
Many, nay, almost any.

Prospero. [Aside]   Honest lord,
Thou hast said well, for some of you there present
Are worse than devils.

Alonso.   I cannot too much muse
Such shapes, such gesture and such sound, expressing—
Although they want the use of tongue—a kind
Of excellent dumb discourse.

Prospero. [Aside]   Praise in departing.

Francisco. They vanish'd strangely.

Sebastian.   No matter, since
They have left their viands behind, for we have stomachs.—
Will't please you taste of what is here?

Alonso.   Not I.

Gonzalo. Faith, sir, you need not fear. When we were boys,
Who would believe that there were mountaineers
Dew-lapp'd like bulls, whose throats had hanging at 'em
Wallets of flesh? Or that there were such men
Whose heads stood in their breasts, which now we find
Each putter-out of five for one will bring us
Good warrant of?

Alonso.   I will stand to and feed,
Although my last: no matter, since I feel
The best is past. Brother, my lord the duke,
Stand to, and do as we.

Thunder and lightning. Enter Ariel, *like a harpy; claps his wings upon the table; and, with a quaint device, the banquet vanishes.*

Ariel. You are three men of sin, whom Destiny—
That hath to instrument this lower world
And what is in't—the never-surfeited sea
Hath caused to belch up you, and on this island
Where man doth not inhabit,—you 'mongst men
Being most unfit to live. I have made you mad,
And even with such-like valour men hang and drown
Their proper selves.

                        Alonso, Sebastian, *&c. draw their swords.*
                    You fools! I and my fellows
Are ministers of Fate. The elements,
Of whom your swords are temper'd, may as well
Wound the loud winds, or with bemock'd-at stabs
Kill the still-closing waters, as diminish
One dowle that's in my plume. My fellow-ministers
Are like invulnerable. If you could hurt,
Your swords are now too massy for your strengths,
And will not be uplifted. But remember—
For that's my business to you—that you three
From Milan did supplant good Prospero;
Exposed unto the sea, which hath requit it,
Him and his innocent child, for which foul deed
The powers, delaying, not forgetting, have
Incensed the seas and shores, yea, all the creatures,
Against your peace. Thee of thy son, Alonso,
They have bereft, and do pronounce by me:
Lingering perdition—worse than any death
Can be at once—shall step by step attend
You and your ways, whose wraths to guard you from
Which here, in this most desolate isle, else falls

Upon your heads—is nothing but hearts-sorrow
And a clear life ensuing.

*He vanishes in thunder; then, to soft music, enter the Shapes
again, and dance with mocks and mows, and carry out the table.*

Prospero. Bravely the figure of this harpy hast thou
Perform'd, my Ariel; a grace it had, devouring.
Of my instruction hast thou nothing bated
In what thou hadst to say. So, with good life
And observation strange, my meaner ministers
Their several kinds have done. My high charms work,
And these mine enemies are all knit up
In their distractions. They now are in my power;
And in these fits I leave them while I visit
Young Ferdinand—whom they suppose is drown'd—
And his and mine loved darling.

Exit above.

Gonzalo. I' the name of something holy, sir, why stand you
In this strange stare?

Alonso.   O, it is monstrous, monstrous!
Methought the billows spoke, and told me of it;
The winds did sing it to me, and the thunder,
That deep and dreadful organ-pipe, pronounced
The name of Prosper: it did bass my trespass.
Therefore my son i' th' ooze is bedded, and
I'll seek him deeper than e'er plummet sounded,
And with him there lie mudded.

Exit.

Sebastian.   But one fiend at a time,
I'll fight their legions o'er.

Antonio.   I'll be thy second.

Exeunt Sebastian *and* Antonio.

Gonzalo. All three of them are desperate: their great guilt,
   Like poison given to work a great time after,
   Now 'gins to bite the spirits. I do beseech you
   That are of suppler joints, follow them swiftly,
   And hinder them from what this ecstasy
   May now provoke them to.

Adrian.   Follow, I pray you.

                                                       Exeunt.

act 4

scene 1. [*Before* Prospero's *cell*]

Enter Prospero, Ferdinand, *and* Miranda

Prospero. If I have too austerely punish'd you,
    Your compensation makes amends, for I
    Have given you here a third of mine own life,
    Or that for which I live, who once again
    I tender to thy hand. All thy vexations
    Were but my trials of thy love, and thou
    Hast strangely stood the test: here, afore Heaven,
    I ratify this my rich gift. O Ferdinand,
    Do not smile at me that I boast her off,
    For thou shalt find she will outstrip all praise
    And make it halt behind her.

Ferdinand.   I do believe it
    Against an oracle.

Prospero. Then, as my gift, and thine own acquisition
    Worthily purchased, take my daughter: but
    If thou dost break her virgin-knot before
    All sanctimonious ceremonies may

With full and holy rite be minister'd,
No sweet aspersion shall the heavens let fall
To make this contract grow; but barren hate,
Sour-eyed disdain and discord shall bestrew
The union of your bed with weeds so loathly
That you shall hate it both. Therefore take heed,
As Hymen's lamps shall light you.

Ferdinand.   As I hope
For quiet days, fair issue and long life,
With such love as 'tis now, the murkiest den,
The most opportune place, the strong'st suggestion
Our worser Genius can, shall never melt
Mine honour into lust, to take away
The edge of that day's celebration
When I shall think, or Phœbus' steeds are founder'd,
Or Night kept chain'd below.

Prospero.   Fairly spoke.
Sit, then, and talk with her; she is thine own.
What, Ariel! My industrious servant, Ariel!

Enter Ariel

Ariel. What would my potent master? Here I am.

Prospero. Thou and thy meaner fellows your last service
Did worthily perform, and I must use you
In such another trick. Go bring the rabble,
O'er whom I give thee power, here to this place:
Incite them to quick motion, for I must
Bestow upon the eyes of this young couple
Some vanity of mine art. It is my promise,
And they expect it from me.

Ariel.   Presently?

Prospero. Ay, with a twink.

Ariel. Before you can say 'come,' and 'go,'
    And breathe twice and cry 'so, so,'
    Each one, tripping on his toe,
    Will be here with mop and mow
    Do you love me, master? No?

Prospero. Dearly, my delicate Ariel. Do not approach
    Till thou dost hear me call.

Ariel.   Well, I conceive.

                                                  Exit.

Prospero. [*To* Ferdinand] Look thou be true. Do not give dalliance
    Too much the rein. The strongest oaths are straw
    To the fire i' the blood: be more abstemious,
    Or else, good night your vow!

Ferdinand.   I warrant you, sir,
    The white cold virgin snow upon my heart
    Abates the ardour of my liver.

Prospero.   Well.
    Now come, my Ariel! Bring a corollary
    Rather than want a spirit: appear, and pertly!
    No tongue! all eyes! be silent.

                                            Soft music.

                    Enter Iris

Iris. Ceres, most bounteous lady, thy rich leas
    Of wheat, rye, barley, vetches, oats, and peas;
    Thy turfy mountains where live nibbling sheep,
    And flat meads thatch'd with stover, them to keep;
    Thy banks with pioned and twilled brims,
    Which spongy April at thy hest betrims
    To make cold nymphs chaste crowns; and thy broom-groves
    Whose shadow the dismissed bachelor loves,
    Being lass-lorn; thy pole-clipt vineyard,

And thy sea-marge, sterile and rocky-hard,
Where thou thyself dost air—the queen o' the sky,
Whose watery arch and messenger am I,
Bids thee leave these, and with her sovereign grace,
Here on this grass-plot, in this very place,
To come and sport:—her peacocks fly amain.
Approach, rich Ceres, her to entertain.

Enter Ceres

Ceres. Hail, many-colour'd messenger, that ne'er
Dost disobey the wife of Jupiter;
Who, with thy saffron wings, upon my flowers
Diffusest honey-drops, refreshing showers,
And with each end of thy blue bow dost crown
My bosky acres and my unshrubb'd down,
Rich scarf to my proud earth—why hath thy queen
Summon'd me hither, to this short-grass'd green?

Iris. A contract of true love to celebrate,
And some donation freely to estate
On the blest lovers.

Ceres.   Tell me, heavenly bow,
If Venus or her son, as thou dost know,
Do now attend the queen? Since they did plot
The means that dusky Dis my daughter got,
Her and her blind boy's scandal'd company
I have forsworn.

Iris.   Of her society
Be not afraid: I met her Deity
Cutting the clouds towards Paphos, and her son
Dove-drawn with her. Here thought they to have done
Some wanton charm upon this man and maid,
Whose vows are that no bed-right shall be paid
Till Hymen's torch be lighted, but in vain.

Mars's hot minion is returned again;
Her waspish-headed son has broke his arrows,
Swears he will shoot no more, but play with sparrows
And be a boy right out.

Ceres.   High'st queen of state,
Great Juno comes; I know her by her gait.

Enter Juno

Juno. How does my bounteous sister? Go with me
To bless this twain, that they may prosperous be
And honour'd in their issue.

They sing.

Juno.   Honour, riches, marriage-blessing,
Long continuance and increasing,
Hourly joys be still upon you!
Juno sings her blessings on you.

Ceres.   Earth's increase, foison plenty,
Barns and garners never empty;
Vines with clustering bunches growing,
Plants with goodly burden bowing.
Spring come to you at the farthest
In the very end of harvest!
Scarcity and want shall shun you;
Ceres' blessing so is on you.

Ferdinand. This is a most majestic vision, and
Harmonious charmingly. May I be bold
To think these spirits?

Prospero.   Spirits, which by mine art
I have from their confines call'd to enact
My present fancies.

Ferdinand.   Let me live here ever;
So rare a wonder'd father and a wise
Makes this place Paradise.

Juno *and* Ceres *whisper, and send* Iris *on employment.*

Prospero. Sweet, now, silence!
Juno and Ceres whisper seriously.
There's something else to do: hush and be mute,
Or else our spell is marr'd.

Iris. You nymphs, call'd Naiads, of the windring brooks,
With your sedged crowns and ever-harmless looks,
Leave your crisp channels, and on this green land
Answer your summons; Juno does command.
Come, temperate nymphs, and help to celebrate
A contract of true love. Be not too late.

Enter certain Nymphs

You sunburn'd sicklemen, of August weary,
Come hither from the furrow and be merry:
Make holiday. Your rye-straw hats put on,
And these fresh nymphs encounter every one
In country footing.

Enter certain Reapers, *properly habited. They join with the*
Nymphs *in a graceful dance, towards the end whereof*
Prospero *starts suddenly, and speaks; after which, to a strange,*
hollow, and confused noise, they heavily vanish.

Prospero. [*Aside*] I had forgot that foul conspiracy
Of the beast Caliban and his confederates
Against my life. The minute of their plot
Is almost come. [*To the* Spirits] Well done! Avoid, no more!

Ferdinand. [To Miranda] This is strange. Your father's in some
passion
That works him strongly.

Miranda. Never till this day
Saw I him touch'd with anger so distemper'd.

Prospero. You do look, my son, in a moyed sort,
As if you were dismay'd. Be cheerful, sir.

Our revels now are ended. These our actors,
As I foretold you, were all spirits and
Are melted into air, into thin air;
And, like the baseless fabric of this vision,
The cloud-capp'd towers, the gorgeous palaces,
The solemn temples, the great globe itself,
Yea, all which it inherit, shall dissolve,
And, like this insubstantial pageant faded,
Leave not a rack behind. We are such stuff
As dreams are made on, and our little life
Is rounded with a sleep. Sir, I am vex'd;
Bear with my weakness; my old brain is troubled.
Be not disturb'd with my infirmity.
If you be pleased, retire into my cell
And there repose. A turn or two I'll walk,
To still my beating mind.

Ferdinand. Miranda.   We wish your peace.

Exeunt.

Prospero. Come with a thought. I thank thee, Ariel: come.

Enter Ariel

Ariel. Thy thoughts I cleave to. What's thy pleasure?

Prospero. Spirit, we must prepare to meet with Caliban.

Ariel. Ay, my commander. When I presented Ceres,
I thought to have told thee of it, but I fear'd
Lest I might anger thee.

Prospero. Say again, where didst thou leave these varlets?

Ariel. I told you, sir, they were red-hot with drinking,
So full of valour that they smote the air
For breathing in their faces, beat the ground
For kissing of their feet, yet always bending
Towards their project. Then I beat my tabor,

At which, like unback'd colts, they prick'd their ears,
Advanced their eyelids, lifted up their noses
As they smelt music: so I charm'd their ears
That, calf-like, they my lowing follow'd through
Tooth'd briers, sharp furzes, pricking goss, and thorns,
Which enter'd their frail shins. At last I left them
I' the filthy-mantled pool beyond your cell,
There dancing up to the chins, that the foul lake
O'erstunk their feet.

Prospero.   This was well done, my bird.
Thy shape invisible retain thou still.
The trumpery in my house, go bring it hither,
For stale to catch these thieves.

Ariel.   I go, I go.

                                        Exit.

Prospero. A devil, a born devil, on whose nature
Nurture can never stick; on whom my pains
Humanely taken, all, all lost, quite lost.
And as with age his body uglier grows,
So his mind cankers. I will plague them all,
Even to roaring.
            Re-enter Ariel, *loaden with glistering apparel, &c.*
Come, hang them on this line.
            Prospero *and* Ariel *remain, invisible. Enter* Caliban,
                Stephano, *and* Trinculo, *all wet.*

Caliban. Pray you, tread softly, that the blind mole may not Hear
    a foot fall: we now are near his cell.

Stephano. Monster, your fairy, which you say is a harmless fairy,
    has done little better than played the Jack with us.

Trinculo. Monster, I do smell all horse piss; at which my nose is
    in great indignation.

Stephano. So is mine. Do you hear, monster? If I should take a
   displeasure against you, look you,—

Trinculo. Thou wert but a lost monster.

Caliban. Good my lord, give me thy favour still.
   Be patient, for the prize I'll bring thee to
   Shall hoodwink this mischance. Therefore speak softly.
   All's hush'd as midnight yet.

Trinculo. Ay, but to lose our bottles in the pool—

Stephano. There is not only disgrace and dishonour in that,
   monster, but an infinite loss.

Trinculo. That's more to me than my wetting, yet this is your
   harmless fairy, monster.

Stephano. I will fetch off my bottle, though I be o'er ears for my
   labour.

Caliban. Prithee, my king, be quiet. See'st thou here,
   This is the mouth o' the cell. No noise, and enter.
   Do that good mischief which may make this island
   Thine own for ever, and I, thy Caliban,
   For aye thy foot-licker.

Stephano. Give me thy hand. I do begin to have bloody
   thoughts.

Trinculo. O King Stephano! O peer! O worthy Stephano look
   what a wardrobe here is for thee!

Caliban. Let it alone, thou fool; it is but trash.

Trinculo. O ho, monster! We know what belongs to a frippery.
   O King Stephano!

Stephano. Put off that gown, Trinculo. By this hand, I'll have
   that gown.

Trinculo. Thy Grace shall have it.

Caliban. The dropsy drown this fool! What do you mean
    To dote thus on such luggage? Let's alone
    And do the murder first. If he awake,
    From toe to crown he'll fill our skins with pinches,
    Make us strange stuff.

Stephano. Be you quiet, monster. Mistress line, is not this my
    jerkin? Now is the jerkin under the line. Now, jerkin, you are
    like to lose your hair and prove a bald jerkin.

Trinculo. Do, do. We steal by line and level, an't like your Grace.

Stephano. I thank thee for that jest; here's a garment for't. Wit
    shall not go unrewarded while I am king of this country.
    'Steal by line and level' is an excellent pass of pate; there's
    another garment for't.

Trinculo. Monster, come, put some lime upon your fingers and
    away with the rest.

Caliban. I will have none on't: we shall lose our time,
    And all be turn'd to barnacles, or to apes
    With foreheads villanous low.

Stephano. Monster, lay to your fingers. Help to bear this away
    where my hogshead of wine is, or I'll turn you out of my
    kingdom. Go to, carry this.

Trinculo. And this.

Stephano. Ay, and this.
    A noise of hunters heard. Enter divers Spirits in shape of dogs and
    hounds, hunting them about; Prospero *and* Ariel *setting them on.*

Prospero. Hey, Mountain, hey!

Ariel. Silver! There it goes, Silver!

Prospero. Fury, Fury! there, Tyrant, there! Hark, hark!
        Caliban, Stephano, *and* Trinculo *are driven out.*

Go charge my goblins that they grind their joints
With dry convulsions; shorten up their sinews
With aged cramps, and more pinch-spotted make them
Then pard or cat o' mountain.

Ariel.   Hark, they roar!

Prospero. Let them be hunted soundly. At this hour
Lie at my mercy all mine enemies.
Shortly shall all my labours end, and thou
Shalt have the air at freedom. For a little
Follow and do me service.

                                                        Exeunt.

act 5

scene 1. [*Before the cell of* Prospero]

Enter Prospero *in his magic robes, and* Ariel

Prospero. Now does my project gather to a head.
My charms crack not; my spirits obey; and time
Goes upright with his carriage. How's the day?

Ariel. On the sixth hour, at which time, my lord,
You said our work should cease.

Prospero.   I did say so,
When first I raised the tempest. Say, my spirit,
How fares the king and's followers?

Ariel.   Confined together
In the same fashion as you gave in charge,
Just as you left them; all prisoners, sir,
In the line grove which weather-fends your cell.
They cannot budge till your release. The king,
His brother, and yours abide all three distracted,
And the remainder mourning over them,
Brimful of sorrow and dismay; but chiefly

Him that you term'd, sir, 'The good old lord, Gonzalo.'
His tears run down his beard, like winter's drops
From eaves of reeds. Your charm so strongly works 'em
That if you now beheld them, your affections
Would become tender.

Prospero.   Dost thou think so, spirit?

Ariel. Mine would, sir, were I human.

Prospero.   And mine shall.
Hast thou, which art but air, a touch, a feeling
Of their afflictions, and shall not myself,
One of their kind, that relish all as sharply,
Passion as they, be kindlier moved than thou art?
Though with their high wrongs I am struck to the quick,
Yet with my nobler reason 'gainst my fury
Do I take part. The rarer action is
In virtue than in vengeance. They being penitent,
The sole drift of my purpose doth extend
Not a frown further. Go release them, Ariel.
My charms I'll break, their senses I'll restore,
And they shall be themselves.

Ariel.   I'll fetch them, sir.

                                                    Exit.

Prospero. [*Makes a circle*] Ye elves of hills, brooks, standing lakes,
    and groves,
And ye that on the sands with printless foot
Do chase the ebbing Neptune, and do fly him
When he comes back; you demi-puppets that
By moonshine do the green sour ringlets make,
Whereof the ewe not bites; and you whose pastime
Is to make midnight mushrooms, that rejoice
To hear the solemn curfew; by whose aid—

Weak masters though ye be—I have bedimm'd
The noontide sun, call'd forth the mutinous winds,
And 'twixt the green sea and the azured vault
Set roaring war; to the dread rattling thunder
Have I given fire and rifted Jove's stout oak
With his own bolt; the strong-based promontory
Have I made shake, and by the spurs pluck'd up
The pine and cedar; graves at my command
Have waked their sleepers, oped, and let 'em forth
By my so potent art. But this rough magic
I here abjure; and when I have required
Some heavenly music—which even now I do—
To work mine end upon their senses that
This airy charm is for, I'll break my staff,
Bury it certain fathoms in the earth,
And deeper than did ever plummet sound
I'll drown my book.

Solemn music.

Re-enter Ariel *before: then* Alonso, *with a frantic gesture,
attended by* Gonzalo; Sebastian *and* Antonio *in like manner,
attended by* Adrian *and* Francisco: *they all enter the
circle which* Prospero *had made, and there stand charmed,
which* Prospero *observing, speaks:*

A solemn air and the best comforter
To an unsettled fancy, cure thy brains,
Now useless, boil'd within thy skull! There stand,
For you are spell-stopp'd.
Holy Gonzalo, honourable man,
Mine eyes, ev'n sociable to the show of thine,
Fall fellowly drops. The charm dissolves apace,
And as the morning steals upon the night,
Melting the darkness, so their rising senses

Begin to chase the ignorant fumes that mantle
Their clearer reason. O good Gonzalo,
My true preserver and a loyal sir
To him thou follow'st! I will pay thy graces
Home both in word and deed. Most cruelly
Didst thou, Alonso, use me and my daughter.
Thy brother was a furtherer in the act.
Thou art pinch'd for't now, Sebastian. Flesh and blood,
You, brother mine, that entertain'd ambition,
Expell'd remorse and nature, who with Sebastian—
Whose inward pinches therefore are most strong—
Would here have kill'd your king; I do forgive thee,
Unnatural though thou art. Their understanding
Begins to swell, and the approaching tide
Will shortly fill the reasonable shore,
That now lies foul and muddy. Not one of them
That yet looks on me, or would know me. Ariel,
Fetch me the hat and rapier in my cell:
I will discase me, and myself present
As I was sometime Milan. Quickly, spirit;
Thou shalt ere long be free.

> Ariel *sings and helps to attire him.*
> Where the bee sucks, there suck I:
> In a cowslip's bell I lie;
> There I couch when owls do cry.
> On the bat's back I do fly
> After summer merrily.
> Merrily, merrily shall I live now
> Under the blossom that hangs on the bough.

Prospero. Why, that's my dainty Ariel! I shall miss thee,
But yet thou shalt have freedom: so, so, so.
To the king's ship, invisible as thou art.
There shalt thou find the mariners asleep

Under the hatches. The master and the boatswain
Being awake, enforce them to this place,
And presently, I prithee.

Ariel. I drink the air before me, and return
Or ere your pulse twice beat.

Exit.

Gonzalo. All torment, trouble, wonder and amazement
Inhabits here. Some heavenly power guide us
Out of this fearful country!

Prospero.   Behold, sir king,
The wronged Duke of Milan, Prospero.
For more assurance that a living prince
Does now speak to thee, I embrace thy body,
And to thee and thy company I bid
A hearty welcome.

Alonso.   Whether thou be'st he or no,
Or some enchanted trifle to abuse me,
As late I have been, I not know. Thy pulse
Beats, as of flesh and blood; and since I saw thee,
Th' affliction of my mind amends; with which
I fear a madness held me. This must crave—
An if this be at all—a most strange story.
Thy dukedom I resign, and do entreat
Thou pardon me my wrongs.—But how should Prospero
Be living and be here?

Prospero. [*To* Gonzalo]   First, noble friend,
Let me embrace thine age, whose honour cannot
Be measured or confined.

Gonzalo.   Whether this be
Or be not, I'll not swear.

Prospero.   You do yet taste
    Some subtilties o' the isle, that will not let you
    Believe things certain. Welcome, my friends all!
[*Aside to* Sebastian *and* Antonio]
    But you, my brace of lords, were I so minded,
    I here could pluck his Highness' frown upon you
    And justify you traitors. At this time
    I will tell no tales.

Sebastian. [*Aside*]   The devil speaks in him.

Prospero.   No.
    For you, most wicked sir, whom to call brother
    Would even infect my mouth, I do forgive
    Thy rankest fault—all of them; and require
    My dukedom of thee, which perforce I know
    Thou must restore.

Alonso.   If thou be'st Prospero,
    Give us particulars of thy preservation;
    How thou hast met us here, who three hours since
    Were wreck'd upon this shore, where I have lost—
    How sharp the point of this remembrance is!—
    My dear son Ferdinand.

Prospero.   I am woe for't, sir.

Alonso. Irreparable is the loss, and patience
    Says it is past her cure.

Prospero.   I rather think
    You have not sought her help, of whose soft grace
    For the like loss I have her sovereign aid,
    And rest myself content.

Alonso.   You the like loss!

Prospero. As great to me as late; and supportable
    To make the dear loss, have I means much weaker

Than you may call to comfort you, for I
Have lost my daughter.

Alonso. A daughter?
O heavens, that they were living both in Naples,
The king and queen there! that they were, I wish
Myself were mudded in that oozy bed
Where my son lies. When did you lose your daughter?

Prospero. In this last tempest. I perceive these lords
At this encounter do so much admire,
That they devour their reason and scarce think
Their eyes do offices of truth, their words
Are natural breath. But, howsoe'er you have
Been justled from your senses, know for certain
That I am Prospero, and that very duke
Which was thrust forth of Milan, who most strangely
Upon this shore, where you were wreck'd, was landed,
To be the lord on't. No more yet of this,
For 'tis a chronicle of day by day,
Not a relation for a breakfast, nor
Befitting this first meeting. Welcome, sir.
This cell's my court: here have I few attendants,
And subjects none abroad. Pray you, look in.
My dukedom since you have given me again,
I will requite you with as good a thing;
At least bring forth a wonder to content ye
As much as me my dukedom.

Here Prospero *discovers* Ferdinand *and* Miranda *playing at chess.*

Miranda. Sweet lord, you play me false.

Ferdinand. No, my dear'st love,
I would not for the world.

Miranda. Yes, for a score of kingdoms you should wrangle,
And I would call it fair play.

Alonso.   If this prove
A vision of the island, one dear son
Shall I twice lose.

Sebastian.   A most high miracle!

Ferdinand. [*Seeing* Alonso] Though the seas threaten, they are
merciful;
I have cursed them without cause.

Kneels.

Alonso.   Now all the blessings
Of a glad father compass thee about!
Arise and say how thou camest here.

Miranda.   O, wonder!
How many goodly creatures are there here!
How beauteous mankind is! O brave new world,
That has such people in't!

Prospero.   'Tis new to thee.

Alonso. What is this maid with whom thou wast at play?
Your eld'st acquaintance cannot be three hours.
Is she the goddess that hath sever'd us
And brought us thus together?

Ferdinand.   Sir, she is mortal,
But by immortal Providence she's mine:
I chose her when I could not ask my father
For his advice, nor thought I had one. She
Is daughter to this famous Duke of Milan,
Of whom so often I have heard renown
But never saw before; of whom I have
Received a second life; and second father
This lady makes him to me.

Alonso.   I am hers.
But O, how oddly will it sound that I
Must ask my child forgiveness!

Prospero.   There, sir, stop:
   Let us not burden our remembrances with
   A heaviness that's gone.

Gonzalo.   I have inly wept,
   Or should have spoke ere this. Look down, you gods,
   And on this couple drop a blessed crown!
   For it is you that have chalk'd forth the way
   Which brought us hither.

Alonso.   I say, Amen, Gonzalo!

Gonzalo. Was Milan thrust from Milan, that his issue
   Should become kings of Naples? O, rejoice
   Beyond a common joy! And set it down
   With gold on lasting pillars: in one voyage
   Did Claribel her husband find at Tunis,
   And Ferdinand, her brother, found a wife
   Where he himself was lost, Prospero his dukedom
   In a poor isle, and all of us ourselves
   When no man was his own.

Alonso. [*To* Ferdinand *and* Miranda] Give me your hands.
   Let grief and sorrow still embrace his heart
   That doth not wish you joy!

Gonzalo.   Be it so! Amen!
         Re-enter Ariel, *with the* Master *and*
            Boatswain *amazedly following*

   O look, sir, look, sir! Here is more of us.
   I prophesied, if a gallows were on land
   This fellow could not drown. Now, blasphemy,
   That swear'st grace o'erboard, not an oath on shore?
   Hast thou no mouth by land? What is the news?

Boatswain. The best news is that we have safely found
   Our king and company. The next, our ship—

Which but three glasses since, we gave out split—
Is tight and yare and bravely rigg'd, as when
We first put out to sea.

Ariel. [*Aside to* Prospero] Sir, all this service
Have I done since I went.

Prospero. [*Aside to* Ariel]   My tricksy spirit!

Alonso. These are not natural events; they strengthen
From strange to stranger. Say, how came you hither?

Boatswain. If I did think, sir, I were well awake,
I'd strive to tell you. We were dead of sleep
And—how we know not—all clapp'd under hatches,
Where, but even now, with strange and several noises
Of roaring, shrieking, howling, jingling chains,
And more diversity of sounds, all horrible,
We were awaked; straightway, at liberty,
Where we, in all our trim, freshly beheld
Our royal, good, and gallant ship; our master
Capering to eye her:—on a trice, so please you,
Even in a dream, were we divided from them
And were brought moping hither.

Ariel. [*Aside to* Prospero]   Was't well done?

Prospero. [*Aside to* Ariel] Bravely, my diligence. Thou shalt be
free.

Alonso. This is as strange a maze as e'er men trod,
And there is in this business more than nature
Was ever conduct of. Some oracle
Must rectify our knowledge.

Prospero.   Sir, my liege,
Do not infest your mind with beating on
The strangeness of this business. At pick'd leisure
Which shall be shortly, single I'll resolve you,

Which to you shall seem probable, of every
These happen'd accidents; till when, be cheerful
And think of each thing well. [*Aside to* Ariel] Come hither,
　spirit.
Set Caliban and his companions free;
Untie the spell.

　　　　　　　　　　　　　　　　　　　　　　Exit Ariel.

How fares my gracious sir?
There are yet missing of your company
Some few odd lads that you remember not.
　　　Re-enter Ariel, *driving in* Caliban, Stephano,
　　　　and Trinculo, *in their stolen apparel*

Stephano. Every man shift for all the rest, and let no man
　take care for himself, for all is but fortune.—*Coragio,*
　bully-monster, *coragio*!

Trinculo. If these be true spies which I wear in my
　head, here's a goodly sight.

Caliban. O Setebos, these be brave spirits indeed!
　How fine my master is! I am afraid
　He will chastise me.

Sebastian.　　　　　　Ha, ha!
　What things are these, my lord Antonio?
　Will money buy 'em?

Antonio.　　　　　　Very like. One of them
　Is a plain fish, and no doubt marketable.

Prospero. Mark but the badges of these men, my lords,
　Then say if they be true. This misshapen knave,
　His mother was a witch, and one so strong
　That could control the moon, make flows and ebbs,
　And deal in her command, without her power.
　These three have robb'd me, and this demi-devil—

For he's a bastard one—had plotted with them
To take my life. Two of these fellows you
Must know and own; this thing of darkness I
Acknowledge mine.

Caliban.   I shall be pinch'd to death.

Alonso. Is not this Stephano, my drunken butler?

Sebastian. He is drunk now. Where had he wine?

Alonso. And Trinculo is reeling ripe. Where should they
Find this grand liquor that hath gilded 'em?—
How camest thou in this pickle?

Trinculo. I have been in such a pickle since I saw you last, that I
fear me will never out of my bones: I shall not fear fly-blowing.

Sebastian. Why, how now, Stephano!

Stephano. O, touch me not—I am not Stephano, but a cramp.

Prospero. You'd be king o' the isle, sirrah?

Stephano. I should have been a sore one, then.

Alonso. This is a strange thing as e'er I look'd on.

> *Pointing to* Caliban.

Prospero. He is as disproportion'd in his manners
As in his shape. Go, sirrah, to my cell;
Take with you your companions. As you look
To have my pardon, trim it handsomely.

Caliban. Ay, that I will, and I'll be wise hereafter
And seek for grace. What a thrice-double ass
Was I, to take this drunkard for a god,
And worship this dull fool!

Prospero.   Go to, away!

Alonso. [*To* Stephano *and* Trinculo] Hence, and bestow your
luggage where you found it.

Sebastian. Or stole it, rather.

Exeunt Caliban, Stephano, *and* Trinculo.

Prospero. Sir, I invite your Highness and your train
　　To my poor cell, where you shall take your rest
　　For this one night, which, part of it, I'll waste
　　With such discourse as, I not doubt, shall make it
　　Go quick away: the story of my life,
　　And the particular accidents gone by
　　Since I came to this isle. And in the morn
　　I'll bring you to your ship, and so to Naples,
　　Where I have hope to see the nuptial
　　Of these our dear-beloved solemnized;
　　And thence retire me to my Milan, where
　　Every third thought shall be my grave.

Alonso.　　　　　　　　　　　　　　　I long
　　To hear the story of your life, which must
　　Take the ear strangely.

Prospero.　　　　　　　I'll deliver all,
　　And promise you calm seas, auspicious gales,
　　And sail so expeditious that shall catch
　　Your royal fleet far off. [*Aside to* Ariel] My Ariel, chick,
　　That is thy charge. Then to the elements
　　Be free, and fare thou well!
　　[*To the others*] Please you, draw near.

Exeunt omnes.

epilogue

Spoken by Prospero

Now my charms are all o'erthrown,
And what strength I have's mine own,
Which is most faint. Now, 'tis true,

I must be here confined by you
Or sent to Naples. Let me not,
Since I have my dukedom got,
And pardon'd the deceiver, dwell
In this bare island by your spell;
But release me from my bands
With the help of your good hands.
Gentle breath of yours my sails
Must fill, or else my project fails,
Which was to please. Now I want
Spirits to enforce, art to enchant,
And my ending is despair
Unless I be relieved by prayer,
Which pierces so, that it assaults
Mercy itself and frees all faults.
As you from crimes would pardon'd be,
Let your indulgence set me free.